NAME YOUR PRICE

Set Your Terms, Raise Your Rates, and Charge What You're Worth as a Consultant, Coach, or Freelancer

KATE DIXON

Oceanside Press • Portland, Oregon

Publisher's Cataloging-in-Publication Data

Names: Dixon, Kate.
Title: Name your price : set your terms, raise your rates, and charge what
you're worth as a consultant, coach, or freelancer / Kate Dixon.
Description: Portland, OR : Oceanside Press, 2021. | Includes index.
| Summary: Guides consultants, coaches, and freelancers on pricing
their services, setting agreement terms, raising rates, and having
meaningful conversations with clients. Topics include: pricing models,
calculating hourly rates, risk factors, financing terms, premiums and
discounts, negotiating with clients, and how to manage mindset.
Identifiers: LCCN 2021920039 | ISBN 9781734699227 (pbk) | ISBN
9781734699234 (ebook)
Subjects: LCSH: Consultants. | Negotiation in business. | Self-em-
ployed. | Wages. | BISAC: BUSINESS & ECONOMICS /
Freelance & Self-Employment. | BUSINESS & ECONOMICS /
Labor / Wages & Compensation. | BUSINESS & ECONOMICS /
Negotiating.
Classification: LCC HD4964.D59 2021 | DDC 331.2 D--dc23
LC record available at https://lccn.loc.gov/2021920039

For Betsy, Will, Jim, Kelly, and Charles

Contents

Introduction

When you think of all the exciting reasons you went into business for yourself, figuring out your pricing and business terms probably aren't the first things on your list. Or even *on* your list.

But maybe they should be.

How you price your services and set the terms in your agreements fundamentally impacts your business' bottom line — and your happiness at work.

I'm a coach and consultant with over nine years of experience running my own practice (and dozens more years working in corporate compensation for great companies), and I've seen things. I've tried things. I've figured out what works for me. And my small business clients have, too.

Part of me thinks I should have titled this book, "All the Things I Learned the Hard Way," but that isn't exactly fair. I learned a couple of them by accident, and a few more through research and benchmarking practices with others. But I will admit that some (many!) of the concepts in the book come from good old-fashioned trial and error.

And that's good news for you! This book will show you all sorts of examples and tips, which will likely shortcut your mistake-making by a country mile. Or ten.

WHAT YOU'LL LEARN

Some of the cool things you'll learn in this book include:

- What **information you need** to figure out how to price your services (and where to get it)
- The **five main pricing models** freelancers and consultants use most
- How to **set your hourly rate**, and how to use it to inform your pricing
- The importance of **showing your clients how to treat you**
- What factors to consider when **pricing your services**, and which **risk factors you can charge more for**
- The most important **terms to include in your agreements**
- Financing terms that can **help you and your client at the same time**
- **What you might (or might not) want to negotiate** with your clients
- Top ways to **manage your energy** so you can be at your best for your customers
- **What to say** (and what not to) in your pricing conversations with your clients
- How to step back and **not take things personally** (it can be done!)
- How to shift your mindset and **get out of your own way**
- When your client (or potential client) needs to be **kicked to the curb**
- How to decide **whether or not to publish your rates**

- …and how to put everything together so you're **at your best** in conversations with your clients!

WHY DO YOU NEED HELP?

A lot of people think they should just be able to figure this out on their own. And some people do. But most of us stumble around, do our best, and are shocked when we hear about how other people conduct their business (both good shocked and bad shocked).

Here are some of the reasons smart, business-savvy people need this book.

How you price your services and the terms in your agreements fundamentally impacts your business' bottom line — and your happiness at work.

You're uncomfortable with the whole pricing thing.

I get it! This isn't your favorite thing to do. And part of the reason could be that you've been shot-in-the-dark-ing things. With this book, you'll get information about pricing models, deciding on your rates, premiums and discounts, and how to raise your prices so you can go into the process with your eyes open.

You don't know what you don't know.

You may not realize the benefits of having certain terms or practices or pricing in place until you're in an uncomfortable situation.

This book will help you learn best practices and teach yourself how to head off some of the worst mistakes…before you make them.

You don't think you deserve higher rates.

Yeah, this is a pretty common issue for people, so you're not alone. But you'll find out why charging more can actually *help* your business (in more ways than one!).

Plus, you'll get tips to get out of your own way, mindset-wise, so you can put those "I'm not worthy!" thoughts to bed.

You've tried things that haven't worked.

While you'll still have to try things to see how they work for your unique business, you'll get tons of tips in this book so you can make an informed decision about how you'd like to move forward.

You know that some of what you're doing isn't right, but you're not sure why.

I'll give you the backstory on why certain things work — or don't. And you can choose tools you'd like to add to your toolbox and which ones to leave behind.

You realize you need help.

Yes, you do! You're not alone in this process — I'll be with you every step of the way.

WHO THIS BOOK IS *NOT* FOR

If you're looking for some sort of chart with specific amounts you should be charging, or if you primarily sell physical products, this isn't the book for you.

Also, if you're looking for a quick fix or "tricks" to use to hoodwink your clients into paying for stuff they don't need, that's not my (or my book's) jam, either.

WHO THIS BOOK IS FOR

If you're a freelancer, consultant, coach, or any other service provider with your own business, I wrote this book expressly with you in mind.

And if you're genuinely curious about how setting your pricing and naming your terms can help you run your service-oriented business better, this is exactly the kind of book that will benefit you.

I love working with inquisitive, hard-working, and self-aware clients to help them get great results for themselves. I wrote this book for people like them!

HOW THIS BOOK IS STRUCTURED

Name Your Price is split into four main sections to make things easy for you:

1. **Toolset.** These are the tools and the information you need to make great decisions about pricing. We'll talk about the difference between freelancers and consultants. We'll take a look at your clients and your value, figure out your hourly rate (even though we won't be using it on its own much), talk about helping your clients know how to treat you, figure out which experts

can help, and give you resources where you can get market data and the other info you need to get started.

2. **Skillset**. You'll find the skills you must develop to price your services well in this section. You'll learn how to use your hourly rate (from the Toolset section) to set prices, look at what risk factors you can charge more for, how to raise your prices and offer discounts, what sorts of terms you need to include in your agreements (and why), the basics of a sales conversation, as well as what to say, and what to avoid at all costs.

3. **Mindset**. This section will help you set your intention for setting your rates, having productive client conversations, and how to get out of your own way. We'll cover shifting your mindset, understanding why you hesitate, and how to not take pricing and contract terms personally. (Which is a bigger deal than you might think.)

4. **Putting It All Together**. You'll learn how to create your game plan around pricing and having conversations about sales, prices, and terms. We'll also talk about when to say "no" to a client, when to revisit your pricing, whether or not to publish your prices, and what to do after you're done with your conversation.

HOW TO USE THIS BOOK

This book is meant to spark ideas and to arm you with knowledge and resources to make great decisions for your business and yourself.

It's not a crutch or a cure-all. It's not a substitute for good judgement, and it can't take into consideration everything that's special about your business, your clients, and your unique situation.

Name Your Price provides insights and actionable steps for pricing your services, setting your terms, and becoming more confident and competent in your conversations with your clients.

Let's get to it!

PART 1

TOOLSET

Your Toolset is the context, information, and tools you need to make great decisions. This covers everything from who you and your clients are, what kind of value you bring, pricing models, how to figure out a foundational hourly rate for yourself, and the basics of helping your clients understand how to treat you.

What's in this section...

Chapter 1: Are You a Consultant or a Freelancer?

How to distinguish between temporary employees, freelancers, and consultants (at least for the purposes of this book).

Chapter 2: Understanding Your Client and Your Value

Defining your niche. Understanding your ideal client. The difference of features and benefits, and why that matters. The role your competition plays. Why and how your client determines the value of your services. Positioning your prices.

Chapter 3: Pricing Models

Understanding the most common pricing models freelancers and consultants use, including hourly rate, value-added packages, consulting proposals, retainers, fractional executive services, and one-to-many services.

Chapter 4: The Foundation: Your Hourly Rate

The benefits and (many) challenges of using hourly rates. Using your hourly rate as a foundation for pricing other types of services.

Chapter 5: Calculating Your Hourly Rate

Different ways to figure out what your hourly rate could be, including a standard approach, double your minimum, and billable hours.

Chapter 6: Data Resources and Reality Checks

How and where to look for competitive service rates in the market. The best way to ask other people in your field for advice. When you should (or shouldn't) care about the market.

Chapter 7: Teach Clients How to Treat You

The importance of helping your clients do the right thing. Modeling great behaviors. How to communicate your expectations. Addressing issues with your clients.

Chapter 8: Your Expert Team

The importance of expert help in your business including your attorney, accountant, other professionals, software and tools.

Chapter 9: Toolset Q&A

Questions I get about topics in the Toolset section (and how I answer them).

Chapter 1

Are You a Consultant or a Freelancer?

A re you a temporary employee, a freelancer, or a consultant? (And why am I asking?)

In order to position yourself appropriately in the market, especially when you're marketing your services to other businesses, it's great to know which category (temp, freelancer, consultant) you relate to best.

These are the definitions I'll be using throughout the book. Just know that you may find differences in these category definitions with different organizations and employers.

TEMPORARY EMPLOYEE

When you're a temporary employee, you may work for a staffing agency (like Kelly Services, Adecco, or Robert Half), or you may work directly for an employer.

Temporary assignments can be of any length, and full- or part-time, but for our purposes, we'll focus on the longer-term (3 to 12 months) ones.

It's typical for the employer to set the hourly rate, or at least a tight range of rates, for these roles, so it's not likely you'll have a ton of room to negotiate your rates (but it never hurts to ask!). And regardless of level, most of these roles are paid hourly, and require you to track the number of hours you work each day.

If you're working a full-time schedule as a temporary worker, you'll likely have access to some sort of benefit coverage, although it's likely to be more expensive and less comprehensive than you'd get with a regular full-time corporate role.

In order to position yourself appropriately in the market, it's great to know which category you relate to best.

Whether you work for an agency or directly for a company as a temporary worker, your employer should be withholding taxes from your paycheck and providing you with a W-2. If this is not the case for the company you're working with, you may be considered a freelancer.

Please know that, while you might find some of the information in this book to be helpful in negotiating your temporary pay rates, this book is primarily designed for freelancers and consultants. If you're planning to move into freelance or consulting work in the future, be sure to read on — you could save yourself a lot of future headaches by setting up your practice intentionally in the first place!

FREELANCER

As a freelancer, you work for yourself, and you may have a single client or more than one. You'll set your own rates, and you'll typically bill your client for the number of hours worked in a given period using your hourly rate (although we'll talk about other ways you can think about billing your services, too). Freelance gigs can vary widely, from just an hour or two up to projects that may take a year or even more.

Freelancers are more likely to be project-focused, and you may work on-site with the client, off-site at your own offices, or a combination of the two.

The most common types of arrangements for freelancers are freelance agreements and retainer agreements. Because you're self-employed, if you're in the United States, you'll typically receive a Form 1099 from your client organization(s), and you'll deal with filing all of your own taxes (and beware: there may be several types of taxes that you'll owe on a local, state, or federal level).

CONSULTANT

When you're a consultant, you typically work for yourself or a consulting practice. For the purposes of this book, we'll assume you're a solo practitioner, although much of the information here can apply to those working in larger practices, as well.

Of course, you may call yourself something different from "consultant" that has meaning in your line of work (like designer, coach, stylist, or facilitator).

Consultants typically work with multiple clients — individuals, organizations, or both. Most work happens away from the client's location; you may even have your own site where clients come to meet you.

As a consultant, you'll likely set your own rates and terms (and may negotiate these with clients). The most common type of arrangements with consultants include value-added packages, consulting proposals, retainer agreements, fractional executive service agreements, and one-to-many services.

If you're working with organizations, you may receive 1099 forms for non-employee compensation (or you may not, depending on the type of engagement). But regardless of the inputs, you or your firm will be on the hook for keeping your books and filing all the applicable local, state, and federal taxes.

PRO TIPS

- Temporary employees, freelancers, and consultants have different pricing, terms, and issues they face. This book focuses on freelancers and consultants.
- Temporary employees don't typically have much leeway to negotiate rates.
- Freelancers typically have more than one corporate client, set their own rates, and they frequently use freelance and retainer agreements.
- Consultants usually work with multiple clients, which can be individuals, organizations, or both. They set their own terms, and use value-added packages, consulting proposals, and retainer agreements.

Chapter 2

Understanding Your Client and Your Value

The first, best thing you can do in your journey to price your services is to get clear on: 1) what you offer, 2) to whom, and 3) the value your services provide to your clients. Lots of people skip ahead to the making-cool-stuff stage (the "build it and they will come" folks), but don't.

Owning a service business implies that you're offering something to someone (or some organization) in exchange for money with certain terms. In this chapter, we're focusing on the *something* and *someone* pieces. The rest of the book deals with pricing and terms, but your work in this chapter is really the foundation everything else is built upon.

YOUR NICHE

As tempting as it is to say that you're in business to help anyone and everyone, that mindset won't serve you well. You need better focus for your business so you can define your value and differentiate your services from those of your competition. And also so you don't go crazy.

Your niche is different from your ideal client (more on that below). Your niche is more aligned with the type of problem you solve. The "something" piece of the puzzle.

Examples include:

When your clients are individuals.

- Resume writing
- Post-trauma Reiki healing
- Designing wills and healthcare directives

When your clients are organizations.

- Helping organizations increase innovation and intrapreneurship
- Consulting with Boards of Directors on executive pay
- Keeping office plants healthy and vibrant

If you haven't done so already, take some time and get clear. It will absolutely help you with your next steps: zeroing in on your ideal clients and the value you provide.

YOUR IDEAL CLIENT

There are zillions of reasons to get clear on who your ideal client is, but we'll be looking from the pricing perspective here. Knowing your client helps you define your value to them, and it can also help you know where to position your pricing.

If you provide services to individuals, it can be a pretty straightforward exercise to come up with a profile that represents your client. I typically refer to these ideal client profiles as "avatars."

If you're working primarily with other businesses, you'll need to think about both the person or team you'll work with most closely and the sponsor of the work, so that might mean you'll create two separate avatars. Some service providers also find it helpful to have an avatar of the business itself.

In any case, if you've had ideal clients in the past, use them for inspirations here. Think about the clients you really like to work with as well as those who get the best results. If there are types of clients you really don't want to serve, jot notes about them, too. Use as much detail as you can (bullet points and phrases work great).

Who are they? This will be the demographics piece. Think about age, gender, income, job, title, and personal characteristics. Or, if you're thinking about an organization, consider revenue size, number of employees, age, industry, location, and values. Get as clear as possible.

What do they want? Make sure you have at least five items on this list. Not all of them will be solved with your services (of course, some absolutely should), but it's great to imagine what goals they have that you can help them tap into. What motivates and drives them?

If you're thinking about an organization avatar, consider profit, purpose, and mission

The client determines the value.

What are they challenged and/or freaked out by? And I don't mean spiders (which may be true, but not relevant, unless you're a pest-elimination service). This is one of the most important pieces of getting to know your clients. If they're worried about something or trying to avoid it, that may point you to a great way to sell your services, or even to create a new service you hadn't thought of providing.

For organization avatars, this could be a bit more challenging. If you've ever done a SWOT analysis (Strengths, Weaknesses, Opportunities, and Threats), this would be the Weaknesses and Threats piece.

What problems will you help them solve? There are the obvious ones (the client will have a new logo) and the less obvious ones (the client will be perceived as more professional). Make sure you're sketching out both.

The more ways you can articulate how your help your clients (organizations or individuals), the better. And keep a running list — as you get to know more and more clients, they will tell you about ways you're helping them that might surprise you.

What kind of results will they get? Some services have easily quantifiable results (client negotiated 18% higher base pay than original offer); some don't. Think about what your clients tell you here, too. Focus on ways your client gets better, stronger, clearer, more effective results, or becomes less stressed, healthier, or more fulfilled.

And yes, you have to write this out (and put it somewhere you can find it again). You'll likely have some brilliant insights as you do this work, and you don't want to lose them!

YOUR VALUE

You don't get to define your value. Your client does that. Say it with me: "The client determines the value." You'll spell out what you *think* your client will get from your time together, but you are not the one who gets to make that final determination.

So, how does the client figure it out, then?

The value of your services is directly connected to how closely your solution meets up with something your client cares about, and either helps them avoid a painful result, or drives an exciting outcome.

The value of your services depends on a combination of two main things:

1. **How effectively your solution addresses their issue.** Most services promise either pain avoidance/relief (figuratively) or pleasure/excitement/fulfillment. Some do both. How does your service do that? As a salary negotiation coach, I help clients avoid feeling incompetent and help them get more pay/benefits/equity from their job offer. And I'm lucky to be able to cite specific dollars and percentage gains to help clients understand the results my clients achieve.

2. **How closely the problem aligns with what they stand for.** Let's imagine your client has a strong family orientation and values higher education, and your services help their kid find and get into their dream college. There's fantastic alignment there, which your client will value.

One of our most important tasks as we sell our services is to help our clients determine the value of our solutions. To do that, we need to show them how effective our services really are.

Share client success stories, or better yet, testimonials with your prospective clients. And by testimonials, I don't mean, "Lisa is awesome!" (which may be true, but it's not specific enough for someone to take action on). Encouraging clients to share specifics about their issue and results can help prospective clients understand — and believe — the value you bring.

Asking for testimonials may feel awkward at first, but they're so supremely valuable for marketing, you owe it to yourself to move out of your comfort zone and make the request.

You also will need to help prospective clients see the alignment between what they care about and what you offer. If you provide dog walking services to busy executives, helping the client see how your service keeps their beloved pet healthy and happy while they're at work could be just the ticket.

It's okay to ask your prospective client, "What would it mean to you if we solved your issue?" In the dog walking example, it could be that the client wants their pet not to feel lonely, or maybe they want to be cuddly with their dog at the end of the day (which wouldn't happen if it didn't get exercise).

Just because the client determines the value doesn't mean you can't help them to see it!

You'll use all of this work over and over again as you build out your website, your marketing materials, and design new services for those awesome ideal clients you've just defined.

POSITIONING YOUR PRICES

Once you know your niche, ideal client, and the value of your services, you can pick positioning that makes the most sense for your business. It's really the combination of all of these things that will point you in the right direction.

Are you in the management consulting field, targeting Fortune 500 clients typically served by big consulting houses? You can target below, at, or above what the big firms charge, depending on the value you provide to the client.

The biggest pricing positioning mistake here, in my mind, would be to price your services far lower than those offered by firms that typically provide them. Your clients will be familiar with those rates and may not take you seriously as a consultant if yours are far below the norm.

That said, if you're a resume writer catering to recent college graduates and you're just starting out, you will likely want to price your services below those for senior executives. You might even position your prices on the lower side of services offered to recent college grads as you establish your business and collect testimonials from clients about the value they're getting from working with you.

But if you have proven expertise in the area you're freelancing or consulting in, be sure you're charging enough for your services. It's almost never a good idea to be a "low price leader." If you struggle in this area, please spend some time with Chapter 18.

Always remember that the amount you charge for the services you provide says something -- to your customer -- about you and your brand.

What I don't recommend is to constantly scan the market so that you can react to it. Sure, it's fine to change your prices, but remember, this is not a contest or some sort of weird day-trading exercise.

PRO TIPS

- Spend plenty of time understanding your ideal clients and the value you provide before you start digging in to pricing your services.
- Narrowing your niche allows you to differentiate your business, focus your efforts, and create a clear target for the right potential clients to find you.
- Truly understanding your ideal client ensures that you design services that appeal to them and helps you market and sell more effectively to them.
- Your clients will decide how valuable your services are to them by evaluating how effectively the service can solve their problem, and how important that problem is to them.

Chapter 3

Pricing Models

There are a number of pricing models used by freelancers and consultants. We'll cover some of the most common arrangements here, but know there are plenty of other models (including hybrids and blends of the ones below).

HOURLY RATE

Using an hourly rate for services is pretty straightforward, and in some types of work, it's "the done thing" (I'm looking at you, attorneys!). With hourly rates, you keep track of the time you're spending, and bill the client for those hours, plus any materials required and other expenses.

So, let me start out by saying I don't love freelancers and consultants using hourly rates with their clients, by and large. Some clients will ask to be billed that way, but there are several reasons I don't think it's a great idea, and I'll get into that in a sec.

We will spend a fair bit of time, though, walking through how to figure out an appropriate hourly rate for yourself (more in Chapters 4 and 5). Why? Because it's the foundation of (or a consideration in) all of the pricing models for services. And sometimes (but rarely!), you just gotta bill hourly.

So…why *not* just go hourly? First of all, your client won't likely have a clue as to how long a job might take, but *you* will (especially after you've been in business for a while).

It's hard for people to buy services when they don't know exactly how much (or even approximately how much) they'll cost.

Next, you may be able to deliver your great results in a shorter timeframe than others doing similar work, which absolutely should *not* be penalized. In fact, I'd argue premium pricing is warranted for it since your speed could provide a benefit to your client.

But the biggest argument I have against using a dollars-per-hour approach is that when you use an hourly rate, it's painfully easy for the client to separate the cost of your fees from the value you're delivering. Which would you rather have a client focus on?

- **Fee focus:** "Nobody's worth $150 (or $300 or $1,000) an hour! That's ridiculous!"
- **Value focus:** "It's definitely worth $500 (or $3,000 or $18,000) to solve my problem."

I rest my case.

RETAINERS

A retainer agreement gives the client a set number of hours over a pre-determined length of time, and specific deliverables are typically undefined (although the range of services *would* be).

Retainer agreements work great for certain types of work, like graphic or product design, as well as legal or financial services. They can also be particularly effective for extending consulting services after you have experience with a client.

FRACTIONAL EXECUTIVE SERVICES

Fractional executive service agreements typically operate much like retainers do, providing the client with a specified number of hours of your time over a set period of time.

Sometimes, fractional executives can also refer to folks who offer full-time, temporary executive work (which shows up more like temporary employee pricing models).

VALUE-ADDED PACKAGES

When you create a value-added package, you bundle products and services together to provide extra value to your client. Like a set of twelve music lessons plus a music book, or four quarterly tax filings plus an update of your accounting program, or six haircuts plus two deep conditioning treatments, or a logo design plus custom stationery and business card layouts.

This bundling does a number of things for you (and your client).

> When you use an hourly rate, it's painfully easy for the client to separate the cost of your fees from the value you're delivering.

Shows your client you know them. When you bundle up services and products that go well together (and are exactly what your client needs), you're demonstrating to your client that you understand them. And the better your customer avatars are (refer back to Chapter 2), the easier it will be to plan perfect packages.

Differentiates your offerings from what others offer. Your carefully curated packages are likely to be different from what your competitors offer, especially when they're going the dollars-per-hour route. Use those differences to your advantage!

Gives your client the full picture. It can be challenging for clients to know how much time they need, so they may mis-estimate the true cost of services billed by the hour. When you offer a package, clients know exactly how much it will cost and what timeframe they can expect.

Makes things repeatable. Creating value-added packages gives you a repeatable way to handle your work so you don't have to reinvent it every time. So awesome.

Allows you to move away from dollars-per-hour. There are tons of reasons for not charging an hourly rate (check out Chapter 4 for details). Packages allow you to articulate your value separately from your pricing, and that is a good thing.

Because of the flexibility value-added packages give you as a freelancer or consultant, I highly recommend exploring this pricing method.

Even professionals who typically bill by the hour can benefit from this approach. The attorney I worked with on estate planning offered value-added packages, which I was delighted to purchase. She knew exactly what I needed, and because her package setup eliminated guesswork on my part, it was easier for me to say "yes."

CONSULTING PROPOSALS

Proposals are the most common way consultants price their services and bill their client organizations. I think of these a bit like custom value-added packages. You come up with an idea to solve for the client's problem, issue, or opportunity, and let the client know what services you'll provide, at what price, and under what terms.

I strongly recommend structuring consulting proposals so that you're pricing deliverables. Just like with value-added packages, pricing deliverables makes it easier for clients to understand the full picture (and easier to say "yes," too).

We'll talk lots more about how to structure consulting proposals and agreements in Chapter 13.

ONE-TO-MANY SERVICES

Another way freelancers and consultants price services is with a one-to-many model where you are the "one," and your clients are the "many." Clients for one-to-many services are almost always individuals instead of organizations, but even when you offer services like these to companies, you will usually do it under the auspices of a consulting agreement.

Offerings like workshops, training courses, masterminds or group coaching, and speaking engagements are all examples of one-to-many engagements.

PRO TIPS

- There are lots of ways to price your services. You don't have to be limited to one way of doing business.
- I don't recommend billing by the hour because it's easy for potential clients to separate your fees from the value you're providing them.
- Value-added packages work great for pricing services since they can show your clients that you "get" them, differentiate you from your competition, and move you away from dollars-per-hour.
- Consulting proposals are a lot like customized value-added packages, and they work well for corporate engagements.
- Retainers are effective for freelancers and consultants alike, and offer clients a reserved number of hours over a period of time.

Chapter 4
The Foundation: Your Hourly Rate

L et me start out by saying I rarely recommend using hourly rates. So why start there?

Your hourly rate really is the foundation for all of your pricing. Whether you have consulting agreements, retainers, workshops, or packages, it's important to have a sense of what you might charge on an hourly basis. Primarily so you don't under-sell yourself.

THE BENEFITS OF KNOWING YOUR HOURLY RATE

It's a shortcut.

You can use it to help price your services.

It's the easiest way to compare what you charge to what your competitors charge. And to be frank, that's both a benefit and a detriment.

WHY NOT USE HOURLY RATES?

There are so very many reasons not to use dollars-per-hour when providing services! Let's review some of the biggest ones.

You don't know how much time you'll ultimately bill.
When you use hourly rates, you don't know how much

time you're committing to. And if you have multiple clients, it's very hard to coordinate your resources among their projects when you don't know how much time to allocate to each one.

Your client doesn't know how much you'll ultimately bill. Having an "open ticket" can be uncomfortable for many clients. They're not quite sure how much everything will wind up costing, and they may conclude that there's no pressure or urgency on you, the provider, to complete the project with an hourly rate type of agreement.

People have preconceived notions about what hourly rates should be. And if yours isn't within that range, they might freak out. Or if they compare your hourly rate as a consultant with what they make per hour (as an employee), they might find the difference distasteful. Because you will need to cover costs for yourself that employees have covered for them by their employer, an hourly rate can seem high, even if it's effectively the same as that of an employee.

It can be challenging to bill for time not spent directly with the client. When you do a lot of preparation, follow up, research, or design for client sessions, the client doesn't see that (or sometimes, appreciate it). And because they don't see it happening, it can be easier for the client to challenge the amount of time or the process you use to get the results that you do.

Don't use dollars-per hour when providing services.

It's harder to add on bonuses or extras. If you want to offer items like worksheets, training, or assessments to your clients, it can be more difficult to get clients to purchase those extras separately. Would you make them free for all your clients? Only for those who meet a certain hourly threshold? How will you value them? This is one of the huge benefits of creating value-added packages (more in Chapter 10).

Your clients may be hesitant to call. If they know they'll be billed for your time, clients might not engage with you when they should. And they may not get the full value of what you can provide because they don't reach out when it would benefit them.

It can encourage client behaviors you don't love. It's not helpful when clients stop focusing on the work you're doing together and start watching the clock. You also don't want to get into negotiating for every single hour ("We only spent 43 minutes this session, so we still have 17 to use at another time").

It may lead to unfair comparisons. Hourly rates are very easy to compare to one another. But they don't tell the full story, especially if you have bonuses or special terms or conditions that you offer and others don't. And frankly, charging an hourly rate makes it easy to compare what you charge to rates for people who are in completely different fields. How should hourly rates for electricians compare to hourly rates for coaches, or stylists, or consultants, or models, or therapists? The answer is: they shouldn't. So don't tempt your clients to do that, either.

HOURLY RATES AS A FOUNDATION

Clearly, you can see I'm not a huge fan of using hourly rates on their own. But you absolutely need to pay attention to hourly rates since they can be an essential element in setting your prices (more in Chapter 10).

So many folks I talk with underprice their services, either because they underestimate what their hourly rate could be or they underestimate the amount of time it takes to provide services (even when they *are* getting paid by the hour).

If you've never tracked your work hours before, I'd encourage you to try it for at least six months. You will almost certainly be surprised at how you actually spend your time! Knowing how long different tasks take to complete can give you much better information on how to price services that are not directly tied to your hourly rate.

PRO TIPS

- Knowing your hourly rate gives you a shortcut to help you price non-hourly services, and it makes it easier to compare your prices to others (which is a double-edged sword).
- There are tons of reasons *not* to use dollars-per-hour when pricing your services, including difficulty for you (and your client) to estimate how much time to allocate, discouraging clients from using your services, and unfair comparisons to hourly rates for other service providers.
- Your hourly rate can be an effective foundation for other types of pricing.

Chapter 5

Calculating Your Hourly Rate

On your journey to discovering what your pricing might look like, I'd recommend using each of these three methods for figuring out a baseline hourly rate figure.

Please note that each method will come up with a different number, and that's okay! We'll talk about what to do with them at the end of the chapter.

These figures are estimations, and they need to be treated as such. There's no such thing as an exact, perfect number to use, and there never will be. These models are meant to be directional guides to help you make some calls on what makes sense for you and your business.

And a quick side-note: I've used a bunch of different examples here to show a variety of hourly rates you might find for different services. One approach isn't better than another just because I used higher numbers in the example!

STANDARD APPROACH

The "standard" approach is to figure out what you'd be paid as a regular, full-time employee doing similar work (including short- and long-term incentives), and bump up the figure to include things that an employer would typically pay on your behalf. Taxes, benefits, facilities, and IT services are all things employers pay for, and they add up quickly!

If you're at a loss for where to start on what the market rate is for the kind of work you do, check out Chapter 6.

I call the hourly rate with no fringe expenses the "gross hourly rate," and the factor you use to increase the hourly rate to comprehend employer-paid items as the "bump up factor."

The equation to calculate gross hourly rate from annual salary is:

$$\text{Annual Rate} \div 2080$$

The figure 2080 is 40 hours per week multiplied by 52 weeks. So, for someone making $41,600, the gross hourly rate would be $20; for someone making $104,000 ($90,000 base + $14,000 target bonus, for example), the gross hourly rate would be $50.

How do you figure out your bump up factor? There's not a perfect number here; you can use whatever you think works best. I recommend 30% as a minimum and moving towards a 40%-50% bump up as long as it doesn't make you feel like throwing up. Here's the formula:

$$\text{Gross Hourly Rate} \times (1 + \text{Bump Up Factor})$$

Using our examples from above, the $20 per hour gross would move up to $26 per hour as a minimum:

$$\$20 \times (1 + .3) = \$26$$

and up to $30 per hour using the 50% bump up rate

$$\$20 \times (1 + .5) = \$30.$$

The $50 gross hourly rate could range from $65 to $75, depending on the bump up factor.

I see consultants and freelancers shortchange themselves on this all the time, primarily because they're not including bonuses and other incentives in their calculation or they're not valuing the employer-provided items that contribute to the bump-up factor at a high enough rate.

DOUBLE YOUR MINIMUM

This method for calculating your hourly rate is super-simple. Just think about the minimum amount you could possibly accept per hour…and double it. Don't think about it too hard, just do it. (Yes, I used to work for Nike.)

If the lowest amount you would possibly accept is $40 per hour, your hourly rate for this method would be $80:

$$\$40 \times 2 = \$80.$$

If your lowest amount is $250 per hour, your hourly rate here would be $500:

$$\$250 \times 2 = \$500.$$

Simple.

BILLABLE HOURS

The billable hours approach allows you to calculate what your rate might be, given the number of hours you expect to bill and the amount of money you would like to make. But before we get to the actual calculation, let's talk about how billable hours work.

The term "billable hours" refers to hours you're working directly on a specific client's behalf.

There are different ways to interpret this — some folks think of it as any work that would not be done if this client engagement didn't exist (which might include travel to and from the client's worksite, creating the client proposal, delivering the services, and billing the client).

It's unrealistic to plan to bill 40 hours per week.

Others only include the service delivery portion. Whatever you decide, be clear, because the different methods will come up with vastly different rates.

Whatever you do in this space, don't estimate booking yourself for 40 billable hours per week. It's not a reasonable expectation. You still have to find work, sell work, and bill work, at a minimum (none of which is billable).

Forget all of those stories you hear of hard-core TV attorneys billing more than 40 hours a week. While you might bill that many hours once in a while, it's not sustainable, and it'll freak you right out with the pressure of achieving it.

Think, too about what "non-billable hours" you need to run your business. Items like doing your taxes, training and development for yourself, marketing, blogging, spending time on LinkedIn, writing proposals, travel time, and networking are all important to your business, but aren't likely to be billable to a client.

And some types of work are much heavier on non-billable hours than others, too, like real estate sales. Whatever you do, don't forget to build in vacation/holiday/sick time into your non-billable hours.

For this calculation, start with your non-billable hours estimate. Let's assume ten days for holidays (80 hours), and three weeks of vacation (120 hours), plus one day a week to do the work of running your business (416 hours). This totals 616 non-billable hours in the year.

Subtract these 616 non-billable hours from the 2080 standard working hours (assumes 40 hours per week), and you have 1,464 hours you can bill.

2,080 Standard Work Hours – 616 Non-Billable Hours = 1,464 Possible Billable Hours

Just an FYI, 1,464 annual billable hours is a lot. A *lot* lot. But let's continue the example. Let's say your goal is to make $100,000 in revenue for the year. Divide that by the number of possible billable hours to see what your minimum hourly rate might be:

$100,000 Revenue Goal ÷ 1,464 Possible Billable Hours = $68.31 Minimum Hourly Rate

But wait! There's more. Notice that I'm calling it a "revenue goal," and not an "income goal." Don't forget that you'll need to pay all of your business expenses out of your revenue, too. That includes all of those pesky things like taxes (federal, state, and local), licenses, software, printing, facilities, certifications, books, website, travel, training, etc.

So, what if we're more conservative with the *possible billable hours*? Of course, that will shift the minimum hourly rate up. Let's look:

$100,000 Revenue Goal ÷ 1,000 Possible Billable Hours = $100 Minimum Hourly Rate

Or if you're more conservative with your *revenue goal*, that will drive your minimum hourly rate down:

$50,000 Revenue Goal ÷ 1,000 Possible Billable Hours = $50 Minimum Hourly Rate

As you can see, there are lots of levers to pull here, but the key is to understand what assumptions you want to make.

Also note that when you're starting up your business, you'll spend a TON more time in the work of running your business than this estimate assumes. Give yourself a break: standing up your business is practically all non-billable, and while it's not a sustainable model over the long-term, it's important to know you'll likely be billable-shy your first few months (at least).

On the other hand, if you've already got an established business, you likely have a good handle on what makes sense for billable hours and revenue goals.

So now that you have estimates using all three methods, what happens next? Take a look, compare and contrast, and see which one feels right. Maybe something in between the three numbers (or above or below them) might sound like an appropriate amount.

Even though you'll probably not use your hourly rate directly with clients, the number you pick to represent it should probably feel a bit daring, but not so crazy-scary that it makes you feel like passing out. If it feels super-comfortable, you might want to push it up a bit to where it does feel a bit more assertive.

PRO TIPS

- There are lots of ways to calculate your hourly rate to use as a foundation for other pricing models, and there is no perfect way to do it.
- The standard approach for calculating an hourly rate converts the annual rate for a regular employee to hourly, then bumps it up by a factor designed to cover expenses typically paid for by an employer.
- If you have a clear idea what a minimum hourly rate you'd be willing to accept, you can double it for an easy way to calculate an hourly rate.
- The most complex method for determining your hourly rate is by determining your desired revenue and dividing it by the number of billable hours you expect to have.
- Because there is no single right answer for what your hourly rate basis could be, it's important to take time to explore different approaches so you can land on something that ultimately feels right to you.

Chapter 6

Data Resources and Reality Checks

I always think it's a good idea to have a sense of what the market is for the type of work you do, and where your pricing stands in the market. Because, like it or not, by accident or on purpose, you're choosing a position within that market.

IT'S NOT GOING TO BE PERFECT

Everyone asks me where they can find pricing data. There's this feeling that if they can just find enough of the right information, the perfect pricing answer will be obvious.

Guess what? It won't.

Because there *is* no perfect price. You have to make a call on what pricing makes sense for you and your clients. And one of two things is likely to happen:

1. You try it, and it doesn't work exactly as you planned, so you have to make adjustments

2. You try it, and while it worked okay at the beginning, as your business changes, you have to make adjustments

Bottom line, don't worry about perfection — you're going to have to change it, anyway. Hope that takes some of the pressure off!

While you don't have to be perfect, you do have to start somewhere, and getting a sense of the market is always a great place to start.

RESOURCES

There are tons of places to get information about freelancing, consulting, and services rates plus full-time salary data (which you can use to help you figure out your hourly rate from Chapter 5).

Regular, full-time salary data. There are lots of great sources of salary data for regular, full-time jobs. Some helpful sites are: salary.com, Glassdoor, payscale.com, h1bdata.info, levels.fyi, and roberthalf.com.

(Hopefully, when you're looking, all of these sites will still be around, but know that some may not be, and there could be newer, cooler sites, too.)

Freelance and consulting rates. Searching for "freelance rates for <whatever it is you do>" will likely be a fruitful activity. Just substitute "consulting" if you're more in that lane. If you want to compare your rates and fees to those of the big consulting firms, a quick search will help you find those, too.

One of the best ways to hone in on the specifics of your industry is by checking out your professional organization's resources. Many of them offer survey data from their memberships, which can be hugely helpful.

Group services. For group services pricing benchmarking, you can search incognito as a customer. Want to know how others price mastermind services? Search the web like a potential client of those services. Same goes for training classes, workshops, or any other group service. Or you may have a sense for pricing because you've been a customer of this type of service before. It's all great input.

Indirect services rates. How you price your indirect services (where you're not actually with your client to provide the service) can be all over the board. As in, literally anything you want, including free.

The good news is that you can do internet searches on just about any indirect service you can think of. But other people's pricing can be all over the place, too, and it can be challenging to figure out the "why" behind their choices. Again, use this as input and information, rather than letting it dictate your prices.

ASKING OTHER PEOPLE

One of the best ways to get information about your pricing is talking with other people, especially people who offer services like yours. But how to ask without sounding weird and stalker-y?

First, make sure the person you're talking with is on board for a conversation like this. Some people just aren't. It might be a scarcity mindset (Chapter 19), or just general discomfort (maybe they're worried they've underpriced the market), but do get them on board before diving into the conversation.

You don't have to justify why you charge what you do.

Let them know you've done your research, and you're hoping to get a read on how well things match up with what they're seeing. You can say something like:

> "According to my research, graphic design free-
> lancers are charging between $X and $Y per hour
> in their retainer agreements. How does that line up
> with what you know of this market?"

It's a lot easier for folks to react to numbers you've found than to have you just ask, "What do you charge?" Don't put them on the spot.

WHY SHOULD YOU EVEN CARE?

Should you even care what other people do? Maybe…but maybe not.

The more unique your offering, the more likely you will be setting the market standard. Which can be both exciting and slightly terrifying. In these situations, you'll be completely on the hook to show your value to your potential clients. But you'll have no constraints about how other people price, so that's nice (or scary, you pick!).

With services that are more common in the marketplace, especially where customers can't easily tell the difference between providers (like in the case of cell phone services), you'll need to know the market. That will help you differentiate what you offer from others, and you can then decide how to position your pricing to reflect those differences.

CREDENTIALS DON'T EQUAL VALUE

There are literally thousands of people who are chasing the next degree or certification or training in hopes of justifying their pricing. Don't do that.

That's not to say that degrees, certification, and training can't help you define value for your client (after all, I have a jumble of letters after my name, and they do come in handy). But don't let them get in the way of doing the hard work of pricing, either.

Just because you have some sort of credential doesn't mean your client will want to pay more. On the other hand, just because you don't have one doesn't mean you're not creating value and worth for your client. Two of the most effective and impactful leadership coaches I know charge a mint (which their clients are delighted to pay), and neither of them has any formal accreditations.

Don't wait to acquire a zillion credentials before raising your prices. If the value is there, the pricing should be, too.

IT'S NOT A RACE TO THE BOTTOM

Trying to be a low-cost leader when you provide services is almost always a losing proposition. With services, it doesn't make sense to compete on price. Compete on value instead, and price accordingly.

Even if you have the lowest prices for the kind of services you offer, be sure that low price provides the right value for the market and clients you want to serve (more in Chapter 2).

For example, if your business is leadership coaching, you might target nonprofit leaders, or first-time managers, or C-suite executives. Each of these client types would require a different value proposition, and you will almost surely price services for each type differently.

And for many types of services, you absolutely can price your offerings too low. Think about it: if you saw a $3 haircut, a $19 business accounting audit, a $4 facial, or a $15 therapy session, how would you react? Skeptically? Me, too.

And if you seek to serve a high-end, executive, luxury, or top-tier corporate clients, low pricing can set off warning bells.

NEVER COMPLAIN; (ALMOST) NEVER EXPLAIN

Don't whine about other people charging more than you do, or having better services than yours, or more clients. It doesn't serve you, and it can wreak havoc on your self-esteem. Besides, it probably isn't even true.

Also? One of the most surprising things for people who are new to pricing their services is that you don't have to justify why you charge what you do.

You *do* have to demonstrate value that supports your pricing, but you don't need to have some sort of a competitive analysis of rates for people doing similar work to you, or any of that sort of thing.

PRO TIPS

- It's great to know what's going on in the market with pricing, but there will never be a perfect number for you to discover, so don't sweat it.
- Much of your pricing research will come from website searches.
- Take the time to see if your professional organization has salary, freelance, or consulting data for your specialty.
- Ask other people to help you get a sense of the market, but don't put them on the spot. That's weird.
- Comparative data may be helpful as you set your prices. But don't get hung up on it, either.
- Your (business) worth isn't defined by the credentials you hold; it's defined by the value you create for your clients.
- Don't make the mistake of pricing your services too low. It can cost you business.
- Whining doesn't help, and you don't need to prove you're charging the "right" amount for your services.

Chapter 7

Teach Clients How to Treat You

Part of our work as freelancers and consultants is to help our clients learn how to treat us, our work together, and our pricing. This is the basis of many of the pricing and terms skills we'll be covering in the Skillset section, so I wanted to cover it here in your Toolset.

CLIENTS DON'T KNOW WHAT THEY DON'T KNOW

Whether it's because they've never worked with someone who provides the type of service you do, or just because they've never worked with someone with your standards and practices, it's a kindness to be clear. Crystal clear. Besides, clarity will be more likely to get you the outcome you're aiming for.

Think back to the first time you used a new service (like getting an oil change, or getting braces, or having a professional file your taxes for you). Chances are good that you had no idea what the etiquette of your new situation was. Where should you wait? How close to your appointment should you brush your teeth? What information should you bring with you? Do you pay before or after the service? Should you tip?

Don't make assumptions that your client will automatically know. Or that what you're expecting is "standard practice." Or that they'll just ask if they have questions (they might, or they might find asking the question embarrassing enough that it makes them run away).

You also don't want your client assuming that you'll handle things the way they're used to doing them. Be clear, be up front, and be sure.

MODEL GREAT BEHAVIOR

One of the best ways to show your clients how to treat you is to model the kinds of behaviors you want to see from them.

Timeliness. If you want your clients to show up on time, always be ready to go at the appointed hour. And if you don't want them always running over their allotted time, make sure you let them know they're getting close to the end of their session, and end on time. This lets your client know that you respect their time and yours, and they should do the same for you.

Preparation. Show your clients how much you value preparation by being prepared and ready to go for any time you spend with them. And when your client has completed work to get ready for your time together, recognize and appreciate it — don't take it for granted.

Cancellations. Prioritize your time with clients on your calendar, and only cancel sessions for absolute emergencies. Be very clear about your cancellation policies for your clients, too, so they know the consequences of cancelling before it happens.

Payments. One of the best ways to ensure that clients pay you in a timely fashion is to bill them in a timely fashion. I've got a vendor whose services I love, but who bills me weeks (and months!) after I use their services. When I finally do get my invoice, it's not top of mind for me, and since I have to go back and figure out what it is they billed me for, it might take an extra few days to get processed.

Modeling good behavior isn't enough, though. You must put your terms, especially around payment, into a written agreement that's signed by both you and your client.

SET CLEAR EXPECTATIONS...IN WRITING

Don't leave things to chance. It's okay if putting your expectations into your agreement or statement of work adds another page to it. And even if you talk with your client about all of your expectations before you start working together, some of it may not soak in until they actually have to do the thing (like rescheduling or paying).

Remember, too, that agreements aren't just about the expectations you have of your clients, but also of what expectations they should have of you. And this goes beyond spelling out the services you will provide. If you have a code of ethics you use, or if you promise to keep your work with your client confidential, bring those into your agreement in writing. Your agreement can (and should) be a reference for your clients.

When you clearly spell out the terms of your agreement (like scheduling, cancellations, pricing, payments, and the like), your clients won't have to guess about the right thing to do. We'll cover this in more detail in Chapter 13.

ADDRESS ISSUES HEAD-ON

This is not the fun stuff. But it *is* important. Crucially so. Even when you're clear about your terms and model great behaviors, sometimes things don't go the way you want or expect them to.

Clients can't get the full value from the work you do together if they don't hold up their end of the bargain.

For example, if a client is late to a session, don't just gloss over it or say that it doesn't matter. It does. And some excuses are ones you're willing to accept, and others aren't. Without a quick discussion, your client may think their behavior is perfectly acceptable. After all, *they're* paying *you*, right?

Get out of the mentality that your agreements to work in a particular way only serve you. Some of them are there to protect you, sure, but many things (like showing up on time) are there for the client's benefit. Clients can't get the full value from the work you do together if they not holding up their end of the bargain (even if they're paying you). Freelance and consulting work is not a one-way street.

I recommend a four-part conversation when things aren't going according to plans.

1. **Be clear about what you expect.** "When clients schedule appointments with me, I'm holding the time open exclusively for them, and I'm expecting them to be there."

2. **Highlight the gap between your agreement and what's happening.** "You cancelled your last session right before our scheduled time, instead of giving me

at least 24 hours notice, which we have in our agreement."

3. **Ask the client for help to resolve the issue.** "What would you recommend to bring things back on track?"

4. **Explain the consequences for things not changing.** "I do give all of my clients one 'free pass,' since I know emergencies do come up. From here on out, though, any cancellations that happen less than 24 hours in advance will be treated as completed sessions."

It can definitely be uncomfortable to address issues with your clients, but when you tackle things head-on, and early in your engagement, there's a far greater chance your client will have great results at the end.

PRO TIPS

- Clients don't always know what's expected of them. Get clear, and you'll have a much better shot at getting the outcome you're looking for.
- One of the best ways to reinforce behaviors you want to see in your clients is to model them yourself.
- Put any important terms, conditions, and expectations in writing; you never know when a client will need to refer to that information.
- If something isn't going according to your agreement, address the issue head-on as soon as it happens. If you don't, your client may think it's okay to behave that way.

Chapter 8
Your Expert Team

W hen you think about pricing and terms and sales, it's easy to slip into the "I can do it all by myself!" mode.

Some of that is likely due to a scarcity mindset (more on that in Chapter 19), where you're trying to keep a lid on costs.

Some of it may be more about wanting to learn all the things, and maybe some could be attributed to avoiding other work in your business that only you can do.

Whatever the reason for the solo mindset, kick it to the curb. You need help. You deserve help. And engaging expert help so you can do your best work is a cost of doing business. Your experts are part of your toolset and are resources you need to get this work done.

A word of caution: don't outsource any work that you're in the best position to do for your business. Things like figuring out your niche, ideal client, and value proposition (more in Chapter 2) all are part of the fundamental and essential "genius work" of building your business. Don't let others make those calls. Even if it's scary. Especially if it's scary, to be honest.

Same with sales and most marketing work. But anything outside of those topics that you don't have the skills or expertise to do is fair game for outsourcing.

Here are some of the most helpful kinds of help in this realm.

YOUR ATTORNEY

Yup! You need an attorney. Whether you're providing services to individuals or to organizations, you need the advice of legal counsel (which I remind you, *I am not*) to help protect you from liability and legal consequences. As a public service announcement, I'm including some things that are a bit outside of the scope of this book.

Engaging expert help so you can do your best work is a cost of doing business.

A few of the things you'll work with your attorney on include:

Setting up your business. Should it be an LLC or a C Corporation (or something entirely different)? How do you navigate a partnership? If you're acquiring a business from someone else, how do you make the transition? Get your attorney's help to do things right.

Writing and reviewing your agreements. While I'll introduce you to some of the concepts for terms to consider including in your agreements, you need a real live attorney to draft and/or review any agreements you sign.

When a company asks you to sign their agreements, you are allowed to "red-line" or edit them — you are not required to sign them as-is. There may be some back and forth, but remember, the word "agreement" implies that both parties agree to it!

Let your attorney help ensure you're agreeing intentionally.

Intellectual property. Attorneys can help you with the patent, copyright, registration, and trademark processes, as well as contracts and agreements so you can protect what you create.

Hiring employees or non-employee workers. There are tons of icebergs to avoid in employment law, and your attorney can help you not be the Titanic.

Entering a commercial lease. You don't want to be in a position where you don't understand what you're agreeing to, so let your attorney help. Commercial leases are complex, and you'd better believe that the person who's leasing to you will know exactly what your (and their) obligations are. You absolutely need to, too.

Attorneys can also do loads more, and depending on the type of work you do, you may need to engage them in other areas, too.

YOUR ACCOUNTANT

Your accountant can be of great help to you in your business in general, but some of the best things in the pricing space include:

Tax implications. The way your business is set up, how you pay yourself (and others), as well as your pricing and billing methods (and timing) may have tax implications. Your accountant can advise you.

Financing terms. If you have a corporate client that expects you to bill them "2/10 net 30," your accountant can help you figure out not only what that means, but how you might want to adjust your pricing to accommodate that payment schedule.

Invoicing and collections. I'm hoping you don't have issues with non-payment (I encourage payment up front wherever possible; more in Chapter 13). But if you do, chances are good that your accountant can help you out. It's great to have someone who's not you reminding your clients to pay on time, and to assist in collecting outstanding bills when needed.

It's great to have a partner in this space!

YOUR SOFTWARE AND TOOLS

I lump software and tools into the "expert" category unabashedly. They help us show up professionally with our clients, which is exactly what the other experts listed here do.

Whether it's an invoicing system, software to help you accept credit cards, an online scheduler, or e-sign software (which might be my favorite business software), it's smart to set up systems and processes that show you're serious about your business. Bonus points if it makes you more efficient, and triple bonus points for anything that makes the client experience better.

One tool I see service providers taking shortcuts with is digital photos, graphics, or other images. Whether you use them on your website, your communications, social media, book covers, or anywhere else, be absolutely sure you have the appropriate rights and make the correct attributions for any images you use. (And if you don't know what your obligations are in thie space, do the research!)

Not only is it the right thing to do, it helps artists get paid appropriately for their work, too.

YOUR OTHER EXPERTS

Insurance agent. In virtually all the service businesses I know, business insurance is a must. Yes, sometimes it can be expensive, and yes, you still need it. Again, it's a cost of doing business.

Web guru. Unless web design is a key part of your service offerings, I recommend hiring someone to help you with your website (and this advice comes from someone who did all of the initial programming of her own site).

Web design and SEO (search engine optimization) are someone else's genius work, and it takes quite a lot of time and effort to keep your expertise up to date.

Assistant. Some people don't find they need assistants to help them in their businesses; others can't live without them. And a third group finds that a bit of temporary help in this area can work wonders.

In any case, it's definitely worth your while to consider if any of the work you do in your business could be done better, faster, and/or cheaper by another resource.

Just about all of your expert advice is considered to be a business expense (but check with your accountant to be sure), and you can view them as table stakes for getting into the business.

If you're having trouble justifying these expenses when you're first getting started, talk with your local Small Business Administration office to see what kind of tools and help they might be able to offer.

PRO TIPS

- Experts (and expert systems) are crucial to running your business in a professional manner.
- Get an attorney. And use them.
- Accountants can provide advice on taxes, financing terms, invoicing and collections.
- Consider your software and tools as experts, too, and don't skimp in this area. You could save untold hours and show up more professionally with the help of great systems.

Chapter 9
Toolset Q&A

Q: I work for a company on a short-term contract. Am I a freelancer or a temporary employee?
A: It depends! The way I think of it, when you get a W-2 or regular paycheck, you're a temporary employee. When you bill your client for your time and services, you're a freelancer (or consultant).

Q: I was talking with my girlfriend about how to price my services, and she says they're too cheap. Should I believe her?
A: Maybe. If your girlfriend uses (or provides) services like the ones you offer, she could offer valuable insights to you. And since most pricing mistakes I see people make are pricing services too low, she may be on to something.

Q: I want to bill my client for a certain number of hours per month. What's the best pricing model to use?
A: I'd suggest looking at either a retainer agreement or a fractional executive services agreement.

Q: How do I know when I've priced my way out of the market?
A: If you have lots of inquiries about your services, but you're not able to win over clients, you'll want to explore your entire sales cycle. It could be an indicator that your prices are too high, or it could be something else, too.

Q: How do I know when my prices are too low?
A: One great indication of your prices being too low is being too busy and/or having too many clients. If you're

priced way too low, though, the opposite can happen —
clients sometimes use price as an indicator of quality, and
they may not see you as a serious expert.

**Q: A friend of mine who does something close to what I
do charges way less. Do I have to meet her pricing?**
A: Absolutely not. Your services and your value are different from everyone else's. Why would you charge the same
as they do?

**Q: What should I do when a client's purchasing depart-
ment requires me to supply an hourly rate?**
A: This sometimes does happen, even if you have an agreement that's not described in hourly terms. I recommend
you ask the purchasing folks what they would use that
number for (if anything), and provide a number with their
use case in mind.

Q: My cousin charges by the hour, so why shouldn't I?
A: Because you're not your cousin. Your business may be
different, and even if it's not, you may want to conduct
your business differently than they do.

**Q: What should I say when a client asks me why I charge
what I do?**
A: Believe it or not, very few clients will ask you about the
how and why of your pricing. You don't need to tell them
how you came up with it or how your prices compare to
others. Shift the focus to the value you provide, and let
them know that your other clients are pleased with their
results.

**Q: How do I differentiate myself from other people who
are doing the same thing as I am?**
A: Value, value, value. When you know who your ideal
client is and what makes them tick, what they want and

need — in a deep and authentic way — you'll put yourself in a great position to stand apart from others who offer similar services.

Q: My client always shows up ten minutes late to our sessions, and that makes me late to my next client appointment. Is there anything I can do about it? I mean, they're paying me...

A: First off, I'd get curious about what's going on with your client. Do they have a standing meeting right before your time together? Would they benefit from a later start time? Ask them.

While it's important to figure out things with your late client, I'm more concerned with *you* being late with your next client.

Since you're showing both your clients how to treat you, I'd recommend finishing on time with your late client, regardless of when they show up. That will hopefully give your first client incentive to start at their scheduled time and allow you to be present for your next client *on time*.

Q: I'm just starting out, and money is tight, so I figured I'll just sign the standard contract from the company I'll be working with. It's okay to do that, right?

A: I wouldn't advise it, no. Bottom line: you and the company you'll be working with have different goals for your agreements. You need to have any contracts or agreements reviewed by a professional who prioritizes *your* interests. Hiring an attorney to help you review and edit agreements is a great investment, especially when you're starting out.

PART 2

SKILLSET

Now, let's talk about your Skillset. These are the skills you need to price your services, set your terms, and have great conversations with your clients.

What's in this section...

Chapter 10: Pricing Your Services

Advice on pricing different types of services, including day rates, retainers, fractional executives, freelance services, consulting services, value-added packages, one-to-many services, and indirect services.

Chapter 11: Risk Factors

How different risk factors could impact your pricing, including client history, speed of turnaround, project scope, customization, and irritation factors.

Chapter 12: Changing Your Pricing

The "why" behind price increases and discounts. Raising your prices and transitioning current clients. Offering price breaks and discounts.

Chapter 13: Establishing Your Terms

What types of terms you may wish to include in freelance agreements, consulting proposals, retainer and fractional executive agreements, direct-to-consumer terms, and financing terms.

Chapter 14: To Negotiate or Not to Negotiate

When to negotiate your rates and terms, and when to skip it. What you can do instead of negotiating.

Chapter 15: The Sales Conversation

Why thought leadership is crucial to landing sales for service providers. How clients make purchase decisions. What to focus on instead of closing the sale. Selling to past clients. The "added extras" approach.

Chapter 16: What to Say...and What NOT to

Sample scripts (both good and bad) for price increases, discounts, premiums, and setting boundaries with your clients.

Chapter 17: Skillset Q&A

Questions I get about topics in the Skillset section (and how I answer them).

Chapter 10

Pricing Your Services

The first of your skills in your Skillset to master is pricing. If you haven't familiarized yourself with the different pricing models, make that your first stop (Chapter 3).

In this chapter, we'll drill down into different models, and leverage your hourly rate to figure out what your stated fees or pricing could look like.

DAY RATE

Not everyone will need to have a day rate, but they can come in handy. You may want to use a day rate if you're offering facilitation or training, if you provide on-site consulting services, or for custom individual services like a stylist traveling to a destination.

Day rates imply that you will be providing services exclusively to the client for the day, and/or that by serving the client in this way, you will be unable to serve other clients.

Your day rate would be a foundation to which you may add other fees. I think of it as the rate for my services without the need for additional preparation or products. For my business, I might use a day rate for a client who wanted to pick my brain about a topic with which I'm very familiar, or to facilitate a group session I'm not providing any content for.

At a minimum, think of your day rate as your hourly rate (see Chapter 5) multiplied by the number of hours in your typical day for the type of engagement. In most office settings, that could mean eight hours; for other types of work, a ten- or twelve-hour day might be more common.

Most clients don't really want to know how you came up with your fees.

Think, too, about how you'd like to treat travel time. Some service providers bill travel time at the same rate as time they're providing services, others bill it at a lower rate, and some don't bill for travel time at all (it's baked into their day rates). There's no single right answer; think about what serves you, your client, and your practice as a whole.

If you prepare a presentation, report, talk, exercises, or training, or if you're using any of your proprietary products or methods, you can — and should! — add fees to your day rate and create a value-added package (more on these later in this chapter).

RETAINER SERVICES

In its simplest form, a retainer agreement is a contract to provide a certain number of hours for a client over the course of a specified amount of time. With retainers, you're typically paid up front or by month (or a combination of the two).

Duration. How long will the term of the retainer be? You can have a lot of flexibility here, but the most common retainers I've seen are between six months and a year.

Number of hours. Again, you have lots of room to play here, but think about what would serve your client best. My preference is to have a limit on the number of hours per month.

Rollover allowance. What happens when a client doesn't use all of their monthly hours? Spell out your rollover policy in your agreement. It's common to allow a portion of the hours to roll over, but not all (although rollover hours are not required).

On one hand, you want to offer flexibility to your client; on the other hand, since you're holding space in your calendar for these hours, you don't want to wind up overcommitted at the end of the engagement, especially if you're balancing the needs of multiple clients.

Hours beyond the retainer. If a client wants to add hours or services beyond what's available to them within the retainer (which could be awesome), it's important to be clear about how you'll handle the situation.

Will you create another proposal for the additional work? Will you simply bill hourly for additional hours (with client approval first)? Spell it out in your agreement to make it easier if and when the situation comes up.

Types of services. It's always good to spell out the types of services you're willing to provide under a retainer. And there are a couple of reasons for that. First, your client may not know all of the ways you could help them, and listing services you provide (even ones they're not currently using) could help you expand your services to them. And if you have any limits or exclusions, it's very important to let them know up front what those are.

To leverage your hourly rate for retainer agreements, you can just plug in your hourly rate and multiply it by the number of hours. Easy-peasy. Or you could add an additional percentage to account for a risk factor (more in Chapter 11).

Or, it could be a bit more complicated. Just don't make it so complex that you can't figure it out or explain your proposal easily! I like to make a few adjustments to my hourly rate to encourage my clients to select more hours over a longer period of time. Both the additional hours and longer duration reduce the risk factors associated with the engagement. You do not have to offer any discount at all, but I wanted to show you what it might look like if you wanted to consider one.

For example, let's say you have both six- and twelve-month retainer durations and allow clients to select either five hours per month or ten hours per month. The total hours for these packages could range from 30 to 120. Your pricing could be 100% of your hourly rate for 30-hour packages, 95% of your hourly rate for 60-hour packages, and 90% of your hourly rate for 120-hour packages. Make sense? Let's do the math, using $100 as the hourly rate:

30-hour package = $100 × 100% × 30 = $3,000 (price for 6-month retainer at 5 hours per month with no discount)

60-hour package = $100 × 95% × 60 = $5,700 (price for 6-month retainer at 10 hours per month OR for 12-month retainer at 5 hours per month with a 5% discount)

120-hour package = $100 × 90% × 120 = $10,800 (price for 12-month retainer at 10 hours per month with a 10% discount)

Don't forget: a big part of successful retainer agreements is communication. Not just up front, when you're putting the agreement in place, but all along the course of the engagement.

You want to make sure that your client feels like they're getting great value from a retainer agreement, and one of the best ways to do that is by letting them know how things are progressing, what you've accomplished, when they have unused or rollover hours, and when their agreement is nearing completion.

For information about retainer services terms, see Chapter 13.

FRACTIONAL EXECUTIVE SERVICES

Fractional executive agreements, designed to give organizations access to a portion of an executive's time, have gained in popularity over the past several years. They can be particularly effective for smaller or start-up companies that can't yet justify investing in a full-time employee at this level, but they do need senior-level expertise and experience.

There are many ways these can be structured, and they typically have some of the features mentioned in Retainer Agreements above. The most common arrangements I've seen in this space put things into the framework of days per month, with four or five as the norm. (Of course, you can create anything you want!)

Part-Time. Think about using your Day Rate to calculate your pricing for being a fractional executive, or use the Standard method to calculate your hourly rate (from Chapter 5) and figure out your pricing from there.

Let's look at an example of a one day per week agreement (we'll use 50 weeks instead of 52 to account for vacations), first with a daily rate of $3,000.

One day per week annual agreement:

1 day × 50 weeks × $3,000 daily rate = $150,000

Now, let's try a two days per month annual agreement, and use an hourly rate of $500.

Two days per month agreement:

2 days × 12 months × $500 per hour × 8 hours per day = $96,000

This type of agreement is especially prone to scope creep, where your client finds other things for you to work on, so be sure to track your hours and communicate with your client as the engagement goes on.

Your client won't always realize how much time they're using, so don't count on them to recognize when they're outside of your original agreement — you'll need to take the lead.

Full-Time Temporary. For any full-time fractional executive engagement, your pricing should reflect a significant premium to the market over a regular, full-time employee.

This premium reflects the higher risk inherent in these types of roles (more on risk factors in Chapter 11). That's the case even if you're paid through the organization's payroll.

As you set your pricing for these engagements, be sure your rate incorporates amounts that reflect short- and long-term incentives (like bonuses and equity grants), which can be substantial at this level. I'd also recommend a bump up factor like we used in the hourly rate calculations in Chapter 5.

For example, here's how we might calculate things for a regular, full-time executive's target base pay of $200,000 with a 40% bonus target and a $100,000 equity grant target:

Regular annual target pay:

$$\$200,000 \text{ base} + (\$200,000 \times 40\%) \text{ bonus} + \$100,000$$
$$\text{equity} = \$380,000$$

Fractional executive annual target pay:

$$\$380,000 \times 1.5 \text{ (bump up factor)} = \$570,000$$

Fractional executive monthly target pay:

$$\$570,000 \div 12 = \$47,500$$

As you can see, adding in bonus and equity targets and using a healthy bump up factor to reflect the risk of the engagement and typically employer-paid benefits and taxes can raise pricing dramatically. Don't be afraid of it!

Whatever method you use, make sure you're creating shared expectations (as well as boundaries) around the number of hours you will work before you begin your engagement.

Make agreements up front about how many hours you'll be working on the client's behalf (including behind-the-scenes work), as well as any standing meetings or specific events you'll be available for.

Chapter 13 has information on terms for fractional executive services agreements.

FREELANCE SERVICES

Most freelancers I know price their services using an hourly rate. If you can move toward offering value-added packages or retainer services (more on both in this chapter), you may be able to more effectively move your pricing up.

If you go with an hourly rate, please refer to Chapter 5 to come up with a figure that will work well for your business.

And check out Chapter 13 where we'll dive into terms and conditions for freelance agreements.

CONSULTING SERVICES

Pricing your consulting services can be tricky at first, especially if you don't have a great understanding of how long it takes to complete tasks. Your experience will build upon itself, though, and it doesn't take many engagements where you underestimate your time to incentivize yourself to get pretty good at it!

In your consulting proposal, you will have sketched out your project deliverables. For each deliverable, estimate the amount of time you will need to complete it (this includes time you'll be directly interacting with your client as well as time you're working on behalf of the client, but not with them). I recommend estimating on the high side for the hours, to accommodate any small shifts and account for unforeseen issues.

Then, add in any costs you have, like special supplies or materials you need, sub-contractor costs, or fees for licensed content or assessments. And that's it!

I like to provide a breakdown by deliverable for the project (typically between three and five deliverables for a multi-month engagement). That gives the client better visibility to what effort goes into the project, and it also allows for negotiating project scope (see Chapter 14).

Let's look at an example of a consulting proposal where your hourly rate is $150, and deliverable 1 is estimated to take 10 hours, deliverable 2 will take 5 hours, and deliverable 3 will take 7 hours.

- Deliverable 1 fees: 10 hours × $150 per hour = $1,500
- Deliverable 2 fees: 5 hours × $150 per hour = $750
- Deliverable 3 fees: 7 hours × $150 per hour = $1,050

Total fees:

$$\$1,500 + \$750 + \$1,050 = \$3,300$$

In my consulting proposals, I don't give my clients the math; I just tell them that fees for Deliverable 1 are $1,500. And if one of the deliverables has added costs or if it's a much more challenging deliverable, you can absolutely shift the fees up to reflect that.

Because you're not showing the clients the underlying math, it's far easier to do. And besides, most clients don't really want to know how you came up with your numbers, and you don't need to defend your fees or break them down for the client, either.

In Chapter 13, we'll talk more extensively about designing consulting proposals and agreements.

VALUE-ADDED PACKAGES

Value-added packages combine services and/or products to create (and show) extra value for your clients. These can be designed for individuals or for group offerings. Factors to consider include:

Duration. How long is the program or package? Your clients will absolutely want to know this. From the pricing perspective, it's related, but not necessarily directly. Sometimes, a package with short duration and high intensity is more challenging to deliver; other times a long-term package is harder to keep going with a client. If one package requires a significant energy boost from you, it could be an indication you might add a premium.

Time spent with you. What kind of direct access will the client have to you, and how much will they get? Is it in person or remote? Is it one-on-one or in a group setting?

Other access to you. Will your client be able to text you between sessions? Email? Slack? Something else? Clients can be all over the map with how much they use this sort of offline service. Some won't contact you at all, but others will be more assertive. Price for the assertive clients.

Features. What kinds of products and services will your client get? This could include training, coaching, treatments, assessments, worksheets, resources, books, audits, or anything else your client values. Make sure you're adding to your pricing for these cool package additions, especially if they take any of your time.

Benefits. Take each thing from your features list, and spell out the reasons it's great for your client. The phrase I use when thinking of benefits is, "and this is awesome, because…" While the benefits won't have a direct impact on your pricing, they do help you establish your value, which may move you to add a pricing premium to your package.

Community. Will you have a way for your client to connect and become a part of a larger community?

Facebook or Slack groups, sharing emails, and doing small group work are all examples of creating community. Again, these are of value to your clients, so be sure to add some sort of fees into your pricing for them.

So, how do you leverage your hourly rate when creating packages? For one-on-one packages, it's a bit simpler than for group packages, so let's start there. We'll cover the group concepts in the one-to-many section below.

Your individual package pricing should almost always be higher than the cost of your time by itself. Depending on the additional services and products you offer, the pricing may be substantially higher.

When you're adding up how much time you're spending, don't forget to include any work you'll be doing on your client's behalf when you're not together (like research, review, interpretation, or design time) as well as access they'll have to you, both direct (in person, phone, video) and indirect (email, Slack, and the like).

Once you've figured out the value of your time, you can add in a figure for the value of the remaining features you're including in your package, and sum everything up. Remember, this is not an exact science, so feel free to play around with different numbers.

Here's an example of a value-added package for a business coach whose hourly rate is $85. The *Better Business Builder* is a three-month package designed to help entrepreneurs start up their new, one-person businesses.

- 10, one-hour coaching sessions: 10 sessions × $85 per hour = $850
- Email access to coach between sessions: estimated 3 hours × $85 per hour = $255
- Worksheets (business plan builder, systems audit, licensing checklist, resource listing): estimated value = $50
- Access to private Facebook group which coach facilitates for 3 months: estimated value = $90

Total price for package:

$$\$850 + \$255 + \$50 + \$90 = \$1,245$$

That number is a basic guideline; you can go higher or lower, depending on your positioning in the marketplace as well as how this package fits with other services you offer.

For information on terms for direct-to-consumer services, see Chapter 13.

ONE-TO-MANY SERVICES

How does your hourly rate come into play for pricing services you offer to groups, like workshops, training courses, and masterminds?

Sometimes, it's a bit of a stretch. But when you figure out your net income (revenue minus costs) for these services, you want to be sure you're earning at least your hourly rate. Sometimes, you can earn lots more, too!

For group packages, the big difference is how you value group time that your clients spend with you (which is not one-on-one). You'll likely want to price group time lower than one-on-one time. And make sure you put a value on any community pieces, as well.

You may have one-to-many services that come together with one-on-one services and indirect services to form a value-added package, too.

Here's an example for pricing a four-hour training class. The venue and catering cost $600, and there are 12 people in the class. Your hourly rate is $120, and you have spent ten hours to prepare and deliver the class.

Costs and pricing:

- Venue: $600
- Class preparation and delivery: 10 × $120 per hour = $1,200

Total costs:

$$\$600 + \$1,200 = \$1,800$$

Class price to break even:

$1,800 total costs ÷ 12 attendees = $150 per attendee

If you raised your prices above $150 per attendee, you could realize more profit. And if you increased the number of attendees, you could also realize more profit.

Be careful about pricing the class below $150 per attendee; at a lower price, you would essentially be working for a lower hourly rate.

INDIRECT SERVICES

While most of what we're covering in the book relates to services that you provide directly (meaning you need to be present to provide the services to the client), some people provide services indirectly (your clients can get the value of the service without you being present), too.

Examples of *direct* services include one-on-one coaching, hair cut and color, logo design, tax filing, or dog walking. *Indirect* services could be things like online courses, newsletters, a video file with a worksheet, an audio guided meditation, a do-it-yourself kit, or access to a cache of articles you've written.

There are plenty of reasons you might want to offer some of your indirect services for lower prices. Indirect services can be a great way for potential clients to experience you before investing in more direct services. You may even want to offer something for free, in exchange for a potential client's contact information.

You can find a lot more information about how others are pricing their indirect services by searching the internet. Pricing for indirect services can be all over the map, so however you decide to price yours, be sure it fits in comfortably with your direct service offerings. And remember: your direct services should always carry higher pricing than your indirect services.

My advice here is to get a general sense of some of the going rates for the types of indirect services you offer, figure out your costs, think about the element's pricing relative to your other offerings, decide your positioning in the market, and try it out. It doesn't have to be perfect, right?

A quick note on free services: you and your business need to be getting something out of anything you offer for free. It might be contact information for your newsletter list, or even getting your name out there as a thought leader, but be very clear about what your goal is and how it relates to your business strategy before you offer something of value for free.

CUSTOM DEALS AND EXCEPTIONS

Before you do custom deals or make exceptions to your regular service offerings, think hard about why you're doing them.

Bad reasons for doing custom deals include:

Because they asked me to. Clients don't always know what would work well for them in their situation. Especially if they haven't used similar services in the past.

Because they can't afford my regular offerings. Your prospective clients may be operating from fear ("I don't think I can afford this, so let me negotiate down to something I feel I can afford"). In most cases where a client uses affordability as a reason to ask for a discount, it's a "value disconnect." The client hasn't rationalized opting in to your offering because they're worried their tradeoff (money and time) won't be worth what they get from your offering.

Because I'm scared to lose them as a client. I hear you… but no. This is classic fear-based mindset (and for more on this, see Chapter 19).

For example, I no longer offer single coaching sessions or allow clients to go session by session. My experience tells me that clients don't get the kind of value and benefits that come with fully committing to the process through one of my carefully crafted value-added packages.

Be the expert and leader that you are. If your experience says that the client won't get the value they need from a custom deal or exception, it's okay to tell them. This happens with potential clients for me on occasion, and I've learned to explain that I can't provide the value they seek in just an hour or two (even if they paid my hourly rate).

There's a reason you set your services up the way you do, and it's perfectly fine if you don't want to set up some sort of custom deal.

But if you do decide to go custom, do it for a *great reason*. Like:

You want to experiment with a new offering. This might be exactly the client and exactly the time to try something new. Especially if you've had it in mind for a while.

You have history with this client. If you've worked with the client before, and you understand how they respond to your services, it may make sense to make an exception. For example, you might add a lesson or session (or two or three) after the end of engagement for a valued client who might not be able to get the full benefit from an additional value-added package.

You know that your current offerings don't fit what this client needs. When the client needs something special from a timing or service perspective, it's certainly fine to create something new. You might find that others could benefit from this new offering down the line, too.

Getting this client has a huge benefit to your business… *beyond* **the financial.** If your potential client is an opinion leader, extends your client base into a new area, or something similarly awesome, it may make sense to offer something custom.

One thing I recommend when you do make an exception is to sit down after you've completed your custom engagement and decide how to handle similar cases in the future. You could decide to stop making this type of exception, continue using this type of exception, or convert your custom deal into a new offering for your practice. Whatever you do, be intentional about it.

PRO TIPS

- Offering a day rate can be helpful for services where you provide services exclusively to a single client for that period of time.
- Retainer and fractional executive agreements can have straightforward pricing, or you could modify your pricing to reflect risk factors in the engagement.
- Value-added packages, one-to-many, and indirect services offer the opportunity to get creative with pricing. Just make sure you don't underprice.
- While you don't want to show your clients your "behind the scenes" pricing math, it's important for you to have a clear estimate of the time you expect to spend on consulting engagements.
- If you decide to create a custom offering or exception to your standard offerings, be sure you're doing it for a reason that enhances your business rather than because you're scared or uncomfortable.

Chapter 11
Risk Factors

Now that you have sketched out pricing for your services, let's look at a few risk factors to consider that might boost (or occasionally reduce) your pricing.

HISTORY WITH THE CLIENT

When you've worked with a client for a long period of time, you have likely created relationships and a foundation of trust you can build on. That makes future engagements less risky — you understand the client's preferences and decision-making processes.

It's also far easier to sell your services to clients who you've worked with successfully in the past who have experienced the value you bring.

On the other hand, engagements with new clients are a bigger risk to you as a freelancer or consultant. There are so many things you don't know about new clients, and getting to know them as you're providing services can be challenging.

You may think that lowering your prices to get a new client would be the most logical path (and there are times where that may be the way to go; see more in Chapter 12).

I would argue that the risks inherent with new clients justify higher pricing. Or at the very least not discounting your prices for new clients.

QUICK TURNAROUND

When clients ask you to produce results with a quicker turnaround time than your standard, that's a risk factor to you. Rush jobs may require you to work in a different way or to use different resources than you typically would.

You may also need to rearrange your work schedule for deliverables you're working on with other clients. And yes, it's easier to make mistakes when you're pulling in a deadline, too.

Quick turnaround times should almost certainly drive some sort of premium pricing. By having an up-charge for rush jobs, you're letting your client know that moving faster than your typical timeline (and moving your client's work to a priority position in your queue) has value to them and that they should pay for that added value.

You can read more about how to add wording about quick turnaround work in Chapter 13.

PROJECT SCOPE

Project scope is one of the places where premium pricing may be justified at either end of the spectrum.

Generally, the shorter the term of engagement, the higher risk it is. Partly because you have to sell a lot more short-term engagements than longer-term engagements to fill your book of business. And if the type of services you offer require proposals and terms negotiation, you're doing a lot of work even before you can get a contract signed. To me, that warrants higher pricing to offset that additional effort.

Larger projects can be more efficient to win, even considering the bigger lift with bidding and selling. On the other hand, the larger the scope of the project, the more eggs you have in a single proverbial basket. If you have an ample history with the client, that can be lower-risk, but a big project with a new client can feel like more of a gamble. The more of a risk to your business a larger project feels like it is to you, the more likely you need to be charging a premium with your pricing.

All other factors being equal, an engagement that calls for a few hours over a short period of time (like two half-day sessions in the course of a week) should be priced higher on a per-hour basis than one that requires more hours over a longer period of time (one day per week for six months, say). Of course, I recommend doing the math in the background, since you almost certainly won't want to share your hourly rate with your clients (more in Chapter 4).

DEGREE OF CUSTOMIZATION

Some of the services you provide, especially offerings you sell directly to individuals, will be largely one-size-fits-all, and no customization will be needed. Your standard pricing can work well here.

But in the event you need to create completely new methods or materials to meet your client's needs, have a plan for premium pricing. This type of work carries higher risk for you than when you're applying practices you have successfully used time and again. Not to mention the additional work you'll need to do to execute and deliver the engagement — both from the client-facing and back office perspectives.

And absolutely, positively charge significantly more when your client will ultimately own the intellectual property (IP) you create. Work with your attorney to ensure your

IP rights are reflected appropriately in your consulting or freelance agreements.

IRRITATION FACTORS

If something really bugs you about working with clients, don't just be irritated about it. Do something about it. Because you can!

There are three main ways you can deal with the irritations that are inevitable when you have a service-oriented business.

Don't do it. If it sets your teeth on edge to work with a particular type of client (or simply a particular client), then don't. Some consultants and freelancers don't like working with nonprofits and will only work with corporate clients; some are the opposite. Maybe you only want to work with individual clients at a certain level in their organization. The great news is that you get to decide. And you may find this helps you define your niche.

> If something really bugs you when you're working with a client, don't just be irritated. Do something about it.

Do it and suck it up. This is my least favorite approach, but there are occasions when it's a must. Just make absolutely sure it's a temporary solution and not a permanent one.

Do it and charge more. If a corporate client has a master agreement that requires you taking a discount in order to be paid in a timely manner, you can raise your prices in order to accommodate that inconvenience to you and your business. Or if a client wants unlimited revisions, charge enough that you can feel good about that practice for them.

There are some irritations that are just too big to bear, though, and you shouldn't have to tolerate bad behavior from clients. Check out Chapter 25 for more on when to just say "no" to working with a client.

HOW MUCH SHOULD RISK FACTORS INCREASE YOUR PRICING?

The amount of premium you elect to charge on top of your regular rates for risk factors is entirely up to you. The question I ask myself in these cases is: "How much extra would I need to make from this engagement in order to feel great about taking on this additional risk?" Sometimes, it's just a percent or two, but sometimes, it can be substantially more.

When the premium becomes significant, it's important to consider whether or not you really want to take on this engagement or client at all. It may not be worth your while.

PRO TIPS

- While it's tempting to lower your prices to win a new client, working with a client for the first time carries its own risk that working with long-term clients doesn't require. The risk that comes from working with new clients needs to, at a minimum, consider whether or not to offer discounts to them.
- Accommodating quick turnaround requests creates risk for you, which you can — and should — charge more for.
- When you create new methods or materials in service of your work with a client, that increases your risk and warrants higher prices.
- It's perfectly okay to charge a premium to deal with things about clients or engagements that bug you.
- The premiums you charge to offset your risks can vary, but when it takes a big pricing increase to make you feel comfortable with the risk of an engagement, stop to consider if it's the right thing to move forward.

Chapter 12
Changing Your Pricing

Setting your prices and understanding the impact of risk factors on your pricing is only the beginning. At some point, you'll need to raise your prices, and you also may want to offer discounts.

The most important piece to understand when changing your prices is why you're doing it.

WHY RAISE PRICES AND CHARGE PREMIUMS?

I support almost every reason freelancers and consultants have for raising their prices and charging premiums.

Why? Because most folks hesitate so much with these decisions, it's not all that common for people to overcharge for their services.

"I just got a new degree/certification/designation"

So, this may sound weird, but your client may or may not care. If you can sell the client on the value of your shiny new qualification, by all means, raise your prices.

"I just feel like it."

Totally legit. My guess is that if you're feeling the need to raise your pricing, there are probably good reasons to do so (the market is changing, your value is increasing), but remember, you don't actually need a reason to raise your prices.

"I'm too busy."

This is a great reason to raise your prices! And while you're at it, you may want to explore ways to "down-sell" clients who will drop out of working with you due to your higher pricing (because they will).

Are there other ways they can experience you through group products or services? There's more on this topic in Chapter 14.

"It's that time of the year."

I can get behind this one, too. And check out Chapter 26 for more on more about when to revisit your pricing.

"My costs are rising."

Sure! That works.

"I'm spending way more time than I thought."

You bet! It's really easy to underestimate the time it takes to work on a project, or prepare for client calls, or whatever it is.

You absolutely should increase your prices when you find out it takes more of your time than you expected to deliver your services.

"Other people are charging way more than I am."

Yes, yes, a thousand times yes!

WHY OFFER DISCOUNTS OR DECREASE PRICES?

I'm much more skeptical about discounts and price decreases than I am pricing higher. And the reason for that is that people sometimes use lower prices for some shady reasons. It's not *always* wrong to discount, though.

"I'm scared/uncomfortable."

If you're offering a discount or decreasing your prices because you're scared to charge what you think you're worth, I'll challenge you to revisit your thinking. Fear is a terrible motivator for pricing decisions. Also? Your pricing probably *should* make you feel at least a little uncomfortable. Not a ton, but a little.

"I want to try out new products or techniques."

Ding ding ding! We have a winner! When you're rolling out a workshop (or other service) for the first time, it's absolutely fine to offer a discount to the first group through (beta testing for the win!). You may find it feels better to not charge full price as you're working out the kinks. Of course, this doesn't mean you have an excuse to roll out a half-baked product.

One of my favorite ways to serve my pro bono/low bono clients is to offer them my new products or services at a reduced price — or even free. It gives me the latitude to experiment a bit while still offering great value to the client.

"I want to land this new client."

We call this "investing in the relationship." And it may be a great reason, or it may not be so super-red hot. Do be up front if you're discounting your prices; you want to make sure the client understands you're doing it on a temporary basis.

"Everybody else is doing it."

This reminds me of a conversation I used to have with my mom (over and over) to justify why I wanted to do something. And of course her response was, "If everyone else is jumping off a cliff, would you do it, too?" Thanks, Mom!

And no. If you're going to discount your prices, make sure it's for a good reason. This isn't one.

"It's for a nonprofit."

Okay…maybe. I've had a fair number of nonprofit clients over the years, and their financial conditions have ranged quite dramatically. Don't automatically assume that a nonprofit client always requires a discount.

"They can't afford it."

You never want to assume you know someone else's financial situation or ability to pay. You don't know if they can afford something or not, to be honest, and both people and organizations invest in what they value.

Don't make an assumption out of the gate that a client won't be able to afford your services. It sometimes does happen, but don't make your prices (and yourself) smaller on a hunch.

Now that you know why you want to do it, let's get into the specifics around raising and discounting your prices.

RAISING YOUR PRICES

Raising your prices can be one of the more challenging pieces of running your business. But you must get comfortable with it — price increases will (and should) come up over and over again.

TIMING

My general rule about the timing of price hikes is "do it whenever it serves you." You don't have to wait for a new year, a new client, a new moon, or whatever else you're waiting for. I know a brilliant career coach who raises her pricing every single quarter. Every quarter. Without fail.

While every three months may not be your cup of tea, there are some moments that are easier and smoother than others to up your pricing.

New year. The beginning of a new year brings the expectation of change, and that little psychological edge can help smooth the way for pricing changes. And don't think strictly of the start of a calendar year; it could also be the beginning of your fiscal year (if it's different than January 1), the start of an academic year, or the beginning of a client's fiscal year.

New clients. It can be easier to implement a new pricing schedule with your next new client. You don't have to explain things to your current clients, which makes things easier (although do see the tips below for transitioning). It can be a little challenging, though, if you are juggling different pricing schedules for different clients, so keep that in mind.

While you can raise your prices anytime, do plan for it, since any changes in your pricing may need to be updated on your website, in marketing materials, or in collateral you share directly with clients.

AMOUNT

Pricing clients ask me all the time about how much they can raise their prices at a time. Is the magic number 5%? 10%? Something higher?

The answer is: it depends. (Of course it does!)

Just like positioning your pricing in the first place (see Chapter 2), the amount you can raise your prices depends on how unique your offer is and the value your clients see in your services.

Raising your prices will likely make you feel at least a little uncomfortable. But you don't need to feel like you're going to lose your mind over it either.

If you're wondering if you're uncomfortable enough with the amount you're raising your prices, sit with the idea for a week or so. When you come back to it, are you a bit more comfortable with it, or markedly less comfortable? If you're feeling a bit better, you've probably picked the right increase. If not, pull back a little on the increase amount, and sit with it again.

If you discover your rates are far below market, don't let an arbitrary increase amount prevent you from moving your rates up substantially. Big increases are the only way to get to where you need to go.

I recently worked with a client who needed to raise her rates by 67% to get into the realm of reality for the type of work she does. That's a gigantic increase, and my client was very uncomfortable at first. But after considering it for a while, she resolved to move forward (and did so successfully!).

TRANSITIONING CURRENT CLIENTS

First of all, be sure to honor the terms of any existing agreement. Winning a price increase at the cost of losing trust isn't a very good bargain.

Whatever your arrangement, it's important to give your clients ample notice that your pricing will be changing. If you can swing it, a 90-day notice period works great, especially for clients who have six- to twelve-month contracts, or those who you only work with occasionally.

Did you know that you can also turn your pricing changes into an opportunity to extend your engagement with your client?

You can offer them an opportunity to get your current pricing for the first three or six months of an annual contract if they renew by the change date.

It feathers in the price change more easily for the client, and you'll still benefit from increased prices over the term of the agreement.

For more information (and mini-scripts) on how to approach conversations with your client about raising your rates, see Chapter 16.

PRICE BREAKS AND DISCOUNTS

Deciding whether and when to offer discounts or free services can be one of the touchiest and most difficult pieces of your pricing portfolio. Get clear on how all of this will work for you and your business. The earlier, the better — this is serious stuff.

BE CLEAR ABOUT IT

When I was applying for my business to become a registered B Corp, one of the things I committed to was to offer a discount to nonprofits serving historically marginalized communities. When I'm pitching to an organization this discount policy applies to, I'm very clear about it in my proposal. (And by "clear," I mean I put the percentage discount into the proposal *in writing.*)

That way, you're establishing your regular pricing with the client from day one. In the event that things change in the future, and you're not willing or able to extend the discount (or if you decide to change it), your client will have a more accurate reference point for your pricing.

PRO BONO AND "LOW BONO"

There may be certain clients or types of clients you decide to offer your services to at no cost or very reduced prices (that's the "low bono" part). This absolutely must be considered a strategic decision for your business — do not wait for a situation to arise where you need to make a call on the fly.

Raising your prices should make you feel at least a little uncomfortable.

Pro bono or low bono engagements should offer some benefit to your business. It may sound mercenary, but it's not — you are making an investment by offering free or discounted services, and your business needs to see some sort of return for that investment.

Those benefits could be anything from goodwill in the community, to beta testing a new service offering, or social proof (testimonials) for your services, or something else. "Just because" isn't good enough.

Planning and articulating your pro bono and low bono strategy can help make your time investments both more intentional and impactful for your business.

WHEN YOUR CLIENT ASKS FOR A DISCOUNT

My experience has been that organizations ask for discounts more frequently than individuals do, but depending on the type of services you offer, you might find things to go the opposite way in your business.

Individuals. If you sell services to individuals, it's likely you'll have some folks approach you for a "friends and family" discount. I've got lots on that coming up in a sec. But what can you do if you have a request for a discount from someone who doesn't fit into your tight social circle?

I recommend holding firm on your pricing, and if you can down-sell, do that instead. Discounting can be a slippery slope, and it can be tough to hold the line on discounting once you start.

You have made deliberate decisions on your pricing and positioning in the market. You absolutely have the right to refuse a request for a discount. To anyone. For any reason.

If every client you talk with is looking for a discount from your regular prices, ask yourself if you are truly connecting with your ideal clients. You may be trying to sell to clients who aren't really ideal, but who may be easy for you to find and attract. Or your marketing or services may not target the people you really want to serve.

Get curious here — this is not an answer that can come in an instant, and the answer can have a profound impact on your business.

Organizations. It's not uncommon for an organization to accept your prices at face value. Occasionally, though, they may request that you reduce the fees for your services.

I find the best way to reduce my pricing for a consulting proposal is to reduce the scope of the services rather than offering a discount on my pricing for the services.

What do I mean by that? Let's say you have four deliverables (of the same size) in your proposal, and your client asks for a 25% discount. I recommend removing one of the deliverables and its fees rather than doing all four deliverables for 25% lower fees. The price will be the same to the client in both cases, but the value of your work will be preserved in the first case.

Even if you only have a single deliverable spelled out, you can use this method — you just need to be specific about how the scope is decreasing (perhaps the offsite meeting facilitation is for a half day instead of a full day), and that everything in the original proposal will not be covered with the reduced pricing.

I always think it's better to negotiate on the scope than the pricing. It puts the focus on the appropriate part of the agreement, and positions your rates as non-negotiable. That way, if the client wants to bring back the piece that you take out of scope, you'll still get paid for it. (This has happened more than once with my corporate clients.)

Another benefit of this approach is that you're demonstrating your flexibility to meet the client's needs without the need to compromise your rates.

"FRIENDS AND FAMILY" DISCOUNTS

If you provide any type of service that your family and/or friends could possibly be interested in, you owe it to yourself to get clear about how you'll handle discounts for those who are closest to you.

In an ideal world, your friends and family would pay full price for your services in order to support your business. And that could absolutely be your policy. It's simple and clear, and totally legit. If you want to deviate from that, figure it out ahead of time so people will know.

When offering this type of discount, you want your friends and family to feel special, but you also don't want their special treatment to come at the expense of the health of your business.

Consider the number of people who might use these benefits as well as the impact serving your friends and family might have on your full-pay clients.

A couple of ideas on how to handle things (some of which aren't discounts at all):

Offer a bonus. For friends and family who buy your services, you could offer a special freebie (like a nail trim when they purchase dog grooming, a business card design with a purchase of a custom logo, or organizing an additional closet when they buy a three-room organizing package).

Provide a discount. Your discount can be whatever you'd like it to be, and you could offer different discounts depending on how close someone is to you (although think about the implications for people finding out they have different discount rates, too).

Service swap. You may have a friend or family member who is interested in your services and who offers services you could benefit from. You could make an arrangement to swap services. Be clear about how this will work, though — you might do an hour-for-hour exchange, or an exchange of similar retail value.

Straight-up free across the board. There are a very small number of people I offer my services to, free of charge. That includes my kids, my siblings, my nieces and nephews, and a couple of best friends. I'm very fortunate to be in a position to do this; you may not be. If you do offer free services, make a list of everyone who is on it (make it a short list!). And stick to it.

When you spell things out ahead of time, you can lean on your policy to be the bad guy. "I offer a friends and family discount of 10%," sounds a whole lot better than, "I'm not really sure <mumble, mumble>." Be firm, consistent, and kind, whatever your decision is in this space.

Don't let friends and family freebies and discounts tank your business — if you can't afford it, you can't, and that's okay. And don't forget to ask for testimonials from friends and family who benefit from your services, too!

RISKS OF PRICE BREAKS AND DISCOUNTS

Price breaks and discounts are a risk to your business. By definition, you don't earn your regular fees in these arrangements, and that can compromise your business' financial health.

Another reason the practice of offering price breaks and discounts can be risky is because you are teaching the client with your every move in this space. When you cave to pressure, you teach your clients that's how to get their discount. But when you have consistent practices and don't discount your prices (and offer flexibility with scope reduction), you're teaching your clients there, too.

Bottom line, offering discounts and free services could compromise the financial success of your business. One of the big risks in this space is not knowing ahead of time how you will handle these requests. Consider exactly how, when, and for whom you would make these special offers before the issue ever comes up.

PRO TIPS

- Raising your prices is a regular part of your business. Get comfortable with it.
- You can raise your rates by any amount you choose, and if you find your current pricing is well below market, you may need to increase them quite a bit.
- Raising your prices should be at least a little uncomfortable, but it shouldn't make you freak out, either.
- Plan well in advance to transition current clients to your new pricing.
- Be crystal clear with your clients that you are offering them a discount.
- Pro bono and low bono engagements are investments for your business that need to bring some sort of return.
- You have the right to refuse requests for discounts from clients.
- A good way to offer lower pricing to a corporate client is to remove deliverables and make a corresponding decrease to the price. Reducing fees for the full set of deliverables devalues your services.
- If you decide to offer friends and family discounts, create a clear policy, including who is included and excluded, before the issue comes up.
- Price breaks and discounts are risky for your business, and in extreme cases may compromise its financial health.

Chapter 13
Establishing Your Terms

Figuring out the terms of your agreements can be even more challenging than figuring out what to charge for your services. Your terms set the stage for how the engagement will go, what you'll deliver, and how you'll get paid.

And always remember Kate's First Law of Terms: *There shall be no surprises for the client.* (At least not if they read the agreements.)

Terms and conditions can look different across the different pricing models and for different types of services. These lists are by no means comprehensive, and you might find items in one model that you'd like to see in a different one. That might indeed work well for your business.

Please know that, like the rest of this book, this section is meant to give you a window into my own experience. **This is NOT legal advice**: *I am not an attorney.* You need your own attorney. You really do. (More about my passion for this topic in Chapter 8.)

What I do hope, though, is that learning a bit about terms and agreements from a layperson's perspective will help you to be more informed. And when you do talk with your own attorney, you can be in a better place to ask questions specifically for you and your own business.

P.S. I'm *still* not an attorney.

Freelance Terms

Freelance agreements are typically much more straight-forward than consulting agreements, and they usually have fewer terms. That said, there are still several terms you — and your client — must be clear on.

HOURLY RATES

Freelance agreements are one of the only places I recommend using hourly rates. But if you don't absolutely have to go hourly, consider using a retainer agreement or value-added packages instead. Even if you wind up using something other than hourly rate to determine your freelance pricing, it's smart to understand the terms that are likely to come up in your agreements.

LENGTH OF ENGAGEMENT

How long will you be working with your client? Freelance agreements can be all over the place, from a week to a year, and everything in between. Because some clients want longer agreements in place just so they don't need to go through the contracting process over and over, it will serve you to get extra-clear on what the client wants from your initial work with them.

Planning your work flow as a freelancer is hard enough without having an unspecified open agreement. Yet another great reason to use another pricing method, if you are able to.

(Side note: if your client wants the engagement to last more than a year, be sure to add a clause in there about revisiting your rates and terms at the one-year mark. Or every six months, if you prefer.)

PLACE OF WORK

Most freelance agreements will specify whether you can work from your own office or if you need to be at their location (and if so, how often). Both arrangements are common, so you'll want to get clear about the client's expectations, and price accordingly. (Which means, if you're required to be onsite with a client, be sure to bake travel time and expenses into your rates.)

EXCLUSIVITY

Occasionally, a client will want you to work exclusively for them, or they will want to restrict your ability in some way to work for other organizations. If you agree to restrictions, your clients should expect your pricing to be higher than if you can work with anyone you choose.

It's helpful to have some sort of wording around client delays and their impact on your prices and service delivery.

Even when a client doesn't restrict your ability to work with others, it's very likely that they will ask you to sign a non-disclosure agreement (NDA).

You will need to understand anything you sign, of course, but pay particular attention to the terms of your NDA to be sure you're staying within the company's guidelines. And if the terms don't work for you, red-line them with your attorney, and see if you can shift them to ones that would be acceptable to you.

OTHER TERMS

Depending on the type of work you do, you may want to clarify other terms and conditions including:

Revisions. Be clear about how many revisions are included in your prices, and what happens if the client wants extras. Will it be a fixed fee or hourly rate? Billed separately, or in addition to the next invoice?

You're doing two things with this practice; first, you're telling your client what "normal" client behavior looks like, and second, you're putting a price on going above and beyond that normal practice. Both are important for your client to understand.

Delays. It's helpful to have some sort of wording around delays on the client side, and how they might impact your pricing and ability to deliver your services. For example, you might want to specify turnaround times as based on the day you receive all required specifications/materials from the client (you can specify what that means, if it's helpful for your type of work), and that required faster turnaround times will incur rush pricing.

Which leads us to…

Rush requests. Clients need to know how you will handle requests for quick turnarounds. (And notice I use the word "request" here — rush jobs should not be a given, unless it is part of how you position your service in the marketplace, and it's built into your pricing.)

Turning work around more quickly than you typically work can be of great benefit to your client, and you should charge a premium for doing so. Set those expectations up front. Wondering how to talk with a client about this topic? Check out Chapter 16.

Intellectual property. You owe it to both yourself and your client to be clear about who owns the intellectual property you are creating. If the client owns it outright, you may want to charge more for your services than if you own it and license it back to the client. This is a fantastic topic to discuss with your attorney, both when you're creating your own freelance agreements and (especially) when you are asked to sign another company's agreement.

Your freelance agreements can be pretty simple and straightforward, but be sure to include all the terms you need to be sure both you and the client understand what happens, when, how, and for how much.

PRO TIPS

- Freelance agreements are one of the few places I recommend using an hourly rate to price your services (although there are great alternatives to using hourly rate for freelancers, too).
- Get clear with your client about their expectations for both the length of the engagement and how much time they expect to spend with you.
- If a client wants to place restrictions on you working with other clients, they should pay for that privilege.
- Specify how revisions, delays, rush orders, and intellectual property rights will be handled in your freelance agreement.

Consulting Terms

I've been working with consulting proposals and agreements for a long time, and I've had the opportunity to see what's worked well, kinda-sorta well, and downright not at all.

It goes without saying (but I'm going to say it, anyway) that you need to engage with your own legal counsel to create the terms and conditions under which you will conduct your business.

My practice is to create a *proposal*, which spells out the "what" of the consulting engagement, and once the client is interested in moving forward, I create a *consulting agreement* with the terms, and an accompanying *consulting addendum*.

Let's break them down.

CONSULTING PROPOSAL

FORMAT

Almost all of my proposals these days are multi-page wonders. I create them in Word and convert them to PDF documents to email to the client. They're in the form of a business letter, even though I can't tell you the last time I actually printed one on paper and sent it through the actual mail.

The goal of the proposal is to provide just enough detail that the client knows how you would approach the work, and they can confidently select you to work with them.

Don't give them so much information that it becomes a project design template for them to use on their own, or worse, with another consultant. (Trust me when I say that it's spectacularly painful to learn that a potential client has made that choice. Ugh.)

In the case of small engagements with clients I've worked with in the past, I'll generally work through the proposal in the body of an email. These can be brief for two reasons: first, they just don't carry a ton of detail, and second, we have a history of working together well in the past and a shared understanding of the way we work together.

In any case, I always cover these four areas:

- Project Overview and Deliverables
- Approach and Timing
- Roles and Meeting Cadence
- Investment

Let's go into more detail.

PROJECT OVERVIEW AND DELIVERABLES

Overview

As an introduction to the proposal, you'll want to recap the problem the client is hoping to solve. They need to know that you understand them. It helps to build rapport, and you'll tie your services back to the problem to make a nice, closed circle.

Take careful notes in your initial meeting with your client — using some of their wording in the overview section can resonate well with your clients. While the length of the problem statement will vary with the size of the engagement, don't spend all of your time on this section: you just need enough detail to let the client know they've been heard, and to support the services you're going to recommend.

Deliverables

Based on the overview, you'll outline three to five key things you'll be delivering to your client. If you've got a major engagement, you could stretch it to seven, but I'd use caution in getting into too much detail.

I like the paragraph headers to be action-y statements, like: "Design and deliver communications plan," or "Collect background data." I'll then follow with a sentence about what we intend to do, and bullets below that with the major outputs (again, three to five works well) for this deliverable.

APPROACH AND TIMING

This section will detail the services, programs, products, and/or deliverables you're recommending to the client. Be clear, and remember to state the features (services) and the benefits. When you're working with a corporate client, the phrase "and this is awesome because…" probably won't be your go-to, but "so that" or "in order to" both work pretty well.

This part of the proposal gives your client a window into how you'll approach the work, with just enough details so they can envision what you'll be doing for and with them. This is the longest section in any proposal.

I like to give them a rough idea of how long each chunk of work will take, too. I've learned to put this into a "Week X - Y" format instead of an actual date format — you very likely won't know exactly when the project will start when you're writing the proposal.

I've had clients dilly dally for weeks (and one that took months!) going through the proposal vetting process. And when you put actual dates in the proposal, clients may get unrealistic expectations of when you can deliver things, even though they're the reason you don't start on time!

ROLES AND MEETING CADENCE

It's important to be clear about who's doing what. Specify who will do project management, meeting agendas, project oversight, and the like.

If you need access to people from the client's organization to be successful, here's where to spell it out. If the organization needs an internal project team, clarify that here, too. For longer-term engagements, I like to request weekly or bi-weekly meetings with the project team (or sponsor, if there's no internal team).

INVESTMENT

Yes, I call it "Investment" instead of "Fees" or "Costing." You can call it whatever you feel comfortable with, though.

When you're having your initial chat with your corporate client, don't hesitate to ask if they have a fixed budget for the project. Because if they do, that can help you both from wasting time. For instance, if a client has a certain budget for a two-day offsite, you can cater your design around what they're able to afford.

Depending on the size of the deliverables, you can either price them separately or just give one price. For larger engagements, I usually break it down by deliverable.

You'll want to specify that some part of the investment is made up front. This is important because you'll be offering your services immediately after signing the agreement. And I've also found that the client is much more focused and aware of time passing once they've made an initial payment.

My practice is to request the entire fee up front for anything under $5,000 USD, and to split the fee 50% up front and 50% upon completion for engagements of $5,000 - $10,000 USD. For larger engagements, I request 30% up front (but am willing to negotiate down to 20-25% if needed), with the remainder split into monthly payments for the expected duration of the contract. But you do you — just get part of your money up front!

You will inevitably run into a situation where your proposal is not accepted. It's a tough pill to swallow when you've invested lots of time preparing and pitching. But it happens, and it's normal.

Until you have signed contracts and received your initial payment, the agreement isn't official.

If you find you're not on the winning end of most of the proposals you pitch, take a step back and seek to understand why. This is a great place to get feedback from a trusted friend who also does consulting work.

CONSULTING AGREEMENT

A consulting agreement spells out the terms for how you'll do your work, and it comes after you've reached a tentative agreement on your consulting proposal.

While the information below works great for some types of work I do (particularly management consulting), it may not be appropriate for yours. I'm hoping it'll give you food for thought and a good jumping-off point.

In any case, you'll want to consult an attorney about how to structure your own agreement. Some companies have standard agreements they want you to sign, and you absolutely *must* have your attorney review (and recommend edits for) every one of them. This is a cost of doing business — *don't be cheap and skip this step*. It could cost you way more in the end.

SERVICES

This is where I spell out what I do, what I don't do, and what the client does. The "I do" part talks about the types of things I do as a part of consulting (like attending meetings, analyzing, reporting on, and making recommendations about things).

The "I don't" piece specifically excludes things (like legal opinions, CPA work, or work typically performed by registered securities broker/dealers). This sets me apart from those types of work that are subject to local, state, and/or federal regulation. These exclusions make sense for my work; you may have different exclusions that apply to your own type of work.

I like to use a "you do" statement in my Consulting Agreements — it's important that clients understand the difference between my role and theirs.

I want it to be clear that I am offering consulting and advice, and they are making decisions about what recommendations they adopt and implement (or not) and how they approach the work.

CONTROL

This section serves to define the relationship of you to the client. It's important to specify that you're operating independently of them, and you have the right to control how your work is performed (including using your own employees or contractors, if you decide it's appropriate).

If it makes sense for your type of work, you could also specify that you're not creating a partnership or joint venture with them through the work you are doing together (unless you are, and then you'd want an entirely different type of agreement).

PROFESSIONAL STANDARDS

You may need something like this; you may not. And some clients care more about having this in writing than others do, too. But here's where I'd drop any statements you'd like to make about "highest ethical and professional standards" and things of that nature.

INSURANCE

Again, some clients want to see a statement about your insurance in your agreement. That might be professional, general liability, or both.

I'm a big believer in having both professional and general liability coverage for my practice. Even though I've thankfully never had cause to use it, I never have to worry about not having it in the unlikely case where I'd need it, either.

CONFIDENTIALITY AND INTELLECTUAL PROPERTY

This is the part where you promise to keep their information confidential (very important to them), and you claim your intellectual property (very important to you).

What's interesting about consulting, which is different from being an employee or even a temporary contract worker, is that you own your work. The organization you're talking with may think it's theirs, but in the United States, it's (almost always) yours. But definitely spell it out. And give your client license to use your materials in whatever way makes sense to you and the organization.

Be specific. Most boilerplate contracts coming from companies will claim anything created by you as a consultant belongs to them, and not only that, they have the right to make money from it. Most consultants I know don't want things to work that way. You must protect your own intellectual property — nobody has as much interest in doing that as you do.

In terms of confidentiality, it's typical for organizations to ask you to keep everything you work on as well as any conversations you have with them confidential.

If you're ever in a position to write or speak about your experiences, you must maintain their confidences, and if you ever want to depart from your original agreement, get it in writing. I ask clients in their post-engagement survey if I may cite their responses, and how to attribute their comments. This clarity pays off!

Depending on the type of work you do, this could be the most important piece of your agreement for you to bring your attorney in to work with you.

FEES AND PAYMENT

This section spells out how much you're charging and when you will bill your clients. And I always include an up-front payment (for more, please see Chapter 13).

My agreements also specify how variable costs like travel, printing, and postage will be paid. I usually create separate invoices for these fees once a month, but do whatever works best for your own business.

It's a great practice to add a phrase into this section that says that fees for any deliverables beyond what are in the services addendum (more later in this chapter) will be quoted and billed separately. It's great to be clear here.

Another thing to think about here is protecting yourself. Until you have signed contracts and receive whatever your initial payment is, the agreement isn't official. Which means you shouldn't be doing work outlined in the agreement.

This provides two advantages to you. First, you're not expending effort on a project that might not move past the planning stages. Second, clients are more motivated to get contracts completed if they can't have you working on their project until agreements are signed.

Again, this is a great example of teaching clients how to treat you.

TERMINATION

It's unlikely, but if you or the client need to end the engagement before it is complete, your agreement should explain how things will be handled.

My agreements typically specify that they can be terminated by either party (me or my client) with 30 days written notice, and that I will prepare a statement of fees and expenses that have already been incurred, and that they're due immediately.

And I let them off the hook for paying fees for services I have not yet provided. Depending on the specifics of your business, you may want different terms here.

CANCELLATIONS

When I do work for a corporate client that involves me being on site or preparing for speaking, team-building, facilitation, or anything similar, I include cancellation terms. So, if the client cancels the event within a certain window (generally, I use a month), I collect half of my fees, and if they cancel within a shorter window (typically a week or two), the client owes me the full fee for the engagement. And if travel is involved, I make sure any fees I've incurred are covered in the event of cancellations, as well.

You can be flexible in this space with the timing and percentage of your fees to collect, but I highly (so highly!) recommend you set some sort of cancellation terms if they are relevant for the kind of work you do.

And in case you were wondering, this is one of the many things in this book I had to learn the hard way. Exactly once.

INDEMNIFICATION AND LIABILITY

This is where your attorney will come in extra-handy. They will have great boilerplate language around holding people harmless, not making claims, not being liable for things, and other stuff that I don't pretend to understand (but opposing counsel absolutely will, if it comes down to it).

Even though I may not fully understand all the phrases and implications thereof (ahem!), it is a great comfort to know that my attorney feels good about my agreement, since they would be required to defend it.

ARBITRATION

Face it. Nobody wants to think about this. At least I don't. But do yourself a favor and add an arbitration clause to your agreement. Your attorney will have one they like to use. Just plunk it in there. Chances are great you won't have to use it, but you'll want it to be there if you need it.

CONSULTING SERVICES ADDENDUM

The consulting services addendum spells out the *what* of your engagement, and works with your consulting agreement (which specifies the *how*).

Don't panic! I know this all seems like a ton of work, but it's really important for you and your client to be on the same page, especially for an engagement that will take months to complete. Besides, most of this content can be pulled over directly from your consulting proposal.

So, why on earth would you need an addendum like this? With my larger consulting engagements, there are usually a few deliverables that get changed, added, or dropped between the time I create the proposal and when we reach an agreement. The services addendum cleans up all of your deliverables, clarifies the timeframe, and puts them into a document that rides along with your consulting agreement.

What's nifty about this approach is that you can create additional addenda if the client wants to add on deliverables, and you don't have to go through the whole agreement process again.

CORPORATE MASTER AGREEMENTS

I wanted to touch on corporate master agreements here. If your client asks you to sign their master agreement without changes, please know that *you do not have to*. At a minimum, take the master agreement to your attorney; it may be acceptable to you, and that's absolutely fine.

But if there are terms in the master agreement that you cannot agree to, work with your attorney to red-line the agreement and see if you can come to terms both you and the client company can live with.

There may be items in the master agreement that the client is unwilling to change (many times, that will include payment terms). Some large companies use this technique to get discounts from their vendors without formally negotiating them.

But instead of being angry about their immovable terms, price your services accordingly. If the company wants you to take a discount in order to be paid within 30 days, move your pricing higher to accommodate that (or even a click more to offset your inconvenience).

If, in the end, you can't get to a point where you can feel good about accommodating their terms, it's okay to walk away. A mismatch isn't a failure. You are not for everyone.

PRO BONO AGREEMENTS

If you think that when you're not charging for your work you don't need to put things in writing, you are wrong. You absolutely should. Anything that helps you and your client to be clear or that protects you and your business needs to be included in your agreement.

PRO TIPS

- Your consulting proposals are the first step in winning consulting business, and they should include just enough detail that the client knows what you intend to deliver and the outlines of your approach to the engagement.
- The consulting agreement spells out how you will approach your work and specifies your terms and conditions.
- The consulting services addendum clarifies the engagement's deliverables and timeframe, and it works with the consulting agreement.
- You don't have to accept corporate master agreements as-is. Always look over them with your attorney, and if you require changes, ask for them. Agreements need buy-in from both sides.
- Consulting agreements are important even when you're not charging for your services. They clarify what you will be doing, and they can help protect you and your business.
- Get an attorney, y'all!

Retainer and Fractional Executive Services Terms

Retainer and fractional executive services agreements are great alternatives when your client wants to reserve a chunk of your time to work with you, but they're not quite sure what they'll have you work on.

These types of agreements are a particularly great choice for clients you've worked with closely in the past. They know you, you know them, and it's easy for you both to see how you could work well together over an extended period of time.

This is as close to dollars-per-hour as I like to get. Sure, your client can back into your hourly rate if they want to, but virtually all retainer clients are organizations (used to dealing with freelance and consulting rates) and not individuals. Retainers also feel different to me since they are agreements to reserve your time, rather than a direct transaction of service and money. They also generally have some sort of payment up front component.

TIME

First, and most importantly for this type of arrangement, you'll want to specify the amount of time a client gets with you. I like to spell out both the total hours as well as the hours per month in this section.

TERM OF ENGAGEMENT

Fractional executive and retainer agreements have a term of engagement, typically somewhere between six and twelve months. They could be shorter, though, especially if the client wants a bigger share of your work hours.

ROLLOVER HOURS

Use your agreement to define what happens to unused hours at the end of each month. Just like rollover minutes with your phone plan, you can have a policy of rolling over a certain number of hours into the next month. You don't have to, of course, but the additional flexibility can be attractive to the client.

One thing I *don't* recommend, though, is allowing the client to have free rein over when they use their hours over the course of the engagement. You could get into a situation where a client doesn't use hours for months, and then wants to use a ton of hours in the last month. That makes planning your work with other clients challenging, to say the least!

When you're clear up front about how hours can expire during the engagement, it's much easier to engage in those discussions. I love retainer agreements, and I want my clients to find them valuable (so they'll renew!). So when a client looks like they won't use all of their hours in a certain month, I let them know, so they don't wind up leaving value on the table.

PAYMENT TERMS

To discount, or not to discount, that is the question. You know I'm pretty skeptical about discounts, but with retainers and fractional executive agreements, I'm a bit more open. In these cases, it's a bit of risk-based pricing (where you charge more for situations that are riskier for you, like we talked about in Chapter 11).

You can offer a discount when a client selects a longer term, or a bigger number of hours, or both. I'd recommend picking either term or hours, though — the double discount can be very challenging to communicate to a client. My personal preference is to offer a modest discount when a client selects a higher number of hours, regardless of the term of the engagement.

There are two main ways to bill for retainer agreements: all up front, or a portion up front with the remainder billed in installments. There's no right or wrong to it, but the larger the total cost of the engagement, the more likely you'll want to bill in installments.

DELIVERABLES

In this section, you'll define what sorts of work you will (and won't) do in the engagement. It's great to show the client all the different things you could be doing with them in the engagement — in my case, that could include everything from program guidance, mentoring junior staff, communications review, quick advice, tie-breaker opinions, and expert analysis. This gives them tons of options beyond what they might initially have in mind. And it could create additional hours or even projects and engagements over time.

Don't expect your clients to set boundaries for you. It's not their job.

Make sure you get in writing what the expectations are beyond just the number of hours you'll make available for them. There may be meetings you need to attend (or lead), progress reports, or other specific deliverables you're signing up for. Get clear on whether these deliverables should be produced within the hours agreed to, or if they're additional (and make sure your pricing reflects any extra work).

When you're doing a fantastic job with your client, it's easy to get scope creep (where your client finds other things they'd like you to work on). While your first inclination may be to just say "yes," you need to be aware of — and protect — your boundaries. Items outside of the scope of your agreement need to be defined and billed separately, which you can do with an addendum to your original agreement. Don't expect your clients to set boundaries for you. It's not their job.

It's smart to be clear up front that hours and deliverables above and beyond what's in the agreement will be scoped and billed separately. You'll help your client avoid surprises, and it'll be easier to bring it up with them if you're in that position.

RENEWALS

Sometime before your agreement expires (I recommend 30 days before for a six-month engagement, and 60 days or more before a year-long engagement), you'll want to schedule a meeting with whoever is sponsoring your engagement.

For these meetings, it's great to show the value that you've delivered to the client so far, and get a read on how the client feels about the engagement. If the tone is upbeat and positive, ask them if they'd like to renew the engagement. You can use incentives to make it easier for the client to agree, if you'd like.

On the other hand, if the tone of the renewal meeting is less rosy, it's smart to address any issues or concerns right away. You can schedule another meeting to ask for the renewal.

DIFFERENCES WITH FRACTIONAL EXECUTIVES

Part-time fractional executives. Fractional executive agreements often work well when a client organization is too small to justify a full-time pay package for a high-powered executive, but they would benefit from that leader's specialized knowledge and expertise. These agreements can look just like other retainer agreements described above.

Full-time, temporary fractional executives. Sometimes, you'll see fractional executive agreements used when a client company wants to temporarily fill a full-time position (typically while they're in search mode for a role, or if they need coverage for an executive's leave).

Special considerations for these types of arrangements include how the engagement may (or may not) be extended, as well as how you would handle an early termination of the engagement.

There are more details on retainer and fractional executive agreements in Chapter 13.

PRO TIPS

- Retainer and fractional executive agreements work well when your client knows they want to work with you, but they're not exactly sure what they want you to work on.
- Offering rollover hours can provide flexibility to your client, but be sure to consider how different client behaviors could impact your other work before setting this term.
- Be sure to give your client ample notice before your agreement expires, and ask for a renewal far enough in advance that your client won't have an interruption in service.
- Part-time fractional executive agreements can look like other retainer agreements, but full-time, temporary ones may need special considerations.

Direct to Consumer Terms

Most of the agreements we've covered so far are Business to Business (B2B): your business is selling to another business. In this section, we'll cover terms for agreements you have directly with the person you're serving. This type of arrangement is Business (you) to Customer (B2C) or "direct to consumer."

The most common types of B2C arrangements are direct services, like one-on-one coaching, consulting, or therapy, and group masterminds or in-person classes. Most of the terms here are intended for direct services.

Indirect services, where you serve your clients without being directly involved (like videos or worksheets or online classes) are common in the direct to consumer space, too.

Many service providers I speak with don't use agreements for B2C work, but they do have other ways they like to communicate terms and agreements. Your clients need to fully understand what they're getting into, and even though you may cover your terms in a discussion, it can be helpful for clients to see things in writing. And to have a document to refer back to.

Talk with your attorney about best practices for the type of work you do — you might find that having your clients sign an agreement with your terms could really benefit you and your business.

PRODUCTS AND SERVICES

With direct to consumer service agreements, the products and services section tends to be the biggest part of the document. I like to include what the client will get, what the client's role in the service is, and what is excluded from our work together.

FEES AND PAYMENT

The fees and payment piece is typically shorter and more straightforward than in consulting agreements. For most of my direct to consumer services, payment up front is required. But for any installment or subscription plans, you must spell out how things will happen (Will you charge the credit card you have on file? What will you do if the payment doesn't go through?).

Your clients need to fully understand what they're getting into.

Of course, you'll want to talk through these terms with your client, too, but be clear in your agreement.

SCHEDULING

For services that require scheduling, it's important to spell out how that should be done as well as how changes will be handled. I have my own clients schedule through an online scheduler (that automatically blocks my busy times), and I allow changes at least 24 hours in advance of the appointment.

Cancellation policies go into this section, too. Specify how far in advance you will accept cancellations, and what will happen if they don't cancel within that window. If you need guidance on how to have a conversation with your client about cancellations, see Chapter 16.

CONFIDENTIALITY

Depending on the type of services you offer, providing a confidentiality statement (where you promise to keep confidential information that's shared with you by the client) can be extremely important.

For my coaching work, I also include a paragraph that highlights that this work is not considered legally confidential (like medical and legal professions), so our communications are not covered by any legal privilege. This may or may not be important to your work.

LIMITED LIABILITY

Just like the services I provide to organizations, I like to include limited liability terms in my service agreements for individuals. My practice is to limit my liability to the amount paid under the agreement, but I recommend working with your own attorney to see what sort of liability statements would work best for your business.

GUARANTEES

Money-back guarantees can be a big help in getting clients to opt in to your services (more in Chapter 13). If you offer one, describe the guarantee in your agreement. Specify how long the client has, what they need to do to request their money back, and your commitment to processing the request. It doesn't have to be long and involved, but your attorney will be able to help you draft clear and concise language here.

COPYRIGHTS AND DISCLAIMERS

While I don't typically talk about copyrights in a direct services agreement, *all* of my collateral pieces (like worksheets, presentations, and blog reprints) have my copyright information on them.

In the case of something larger, like a course, book, or workbook I might offer to clients, I also include disclaimers and more information about exactly how people can (short quotations in reviews or non-commercial uses) and cannot (basically everything else) be reproduced, shared, transmitted or sold.

Your attorney can help you craft a great disclaimer and other usage rights language.

PRO TIPS

- The terms you include in your agreements with individuals may be different from ones you use with other businesses.
- Clients need to clearly and fully understand what they are agreeing to.
- Some terms will be more important than others for the types of services you offer.
- Your attorney can help you draft terms and conditions and advise you on best practices to share them with your clients.

Financing Terms

How you require and accept payments can be some of the most crucial decisions you make about your business. They can impact whether you close a sale, how fast a client pays you, and whether they pay you on time (or at all).

Financing terms can also be some of the most frustrating parts of running your business. But if you're frustrated, it's just the universe telling you that you need some sort of policy or practice — defined up front — that either prevents it from happening, or provides you extra money so you can afford not to worry about it.

PAY UP FRONT

I ask my individual clients to pay me up front for all except the very largest packages. Why? It's easier on the client and easier on me. For the client, once they pay, they can focus on the service, and never worry about it again. You don't want to put them through a decision moment about payment every single month.

From my perspective, I love just billing once, instead of having to invoice a client multiple times (along with any follow up for slow payers). There is a risk to you in having multiple payments, too; the client may not be able or willing to pay down the road.

With large individual packages and smaller consulting agreements, I typically require an up-front payment of 50%.

For my corporate clients, I ask for an up front payment somewhere between 20% and 50%, depending on the size of the engagement (smaller engagements require larger deposits and vice versa).

When I first started out, I didn't put such an emphasis on these initial payments. I discovered, though, that clients who pay up front (or make a substantial deposit) engage in the work we do together much more quickly and enthusiastically. There's something almost magical about it — that feeling of investing in themselves or their project immediately creates focus and energy.

The practice of paying up front really does benefit both you and your client.

PAYMENT PLANS

My clients sometimes fret over charging their clients more for a payment plan than they would for a single, paid-up-front payment. Don't. Payment plans are a convenience for them, and while it's a bit of a pain for you, the real issue is that it's more of a risk to you when you're not getting paid up front.

My recommendation is that you charge between a 10% and 20% premium for any financing or payment plans you offer. While there's no set rule about how much to collect for the first payment (which I make due before services start), I generally recommend a 50% up-front payment.

I also think it's riskier to extend payment plans past the time the client is receiving services (like offering a payment plan of 12 months for a 6-month package), so I recommend that the last payment be due no later than the last date of service.

Do yourself a favor here, too: if your invoicing software allows you to set up your payment plan invoices to auto-send for the duration of the plan, *do it*. You don't want to be in the system at the top of every month managing every payment manually.

SUBSCRIPTIONS

Subscription plans are great for certain types of services, like memberships or masterminds.

How you require and accept payments can be some of the most crucial decisions you make about your business.

Whatever you do, though, be sure to give plenty of notice that you're renewing. In the case of an annual or semi-annual subscription, be sure to let your client know that there's an upcoming auto-renewal, and that if they would like to change their credit card information, to do it before the renewal.

There's nothing quite as frustrating as seeing a "thanks for renewing your subscription" when you didn't intend to. As a customer, I personally find it to be infuriating. I've even asked for a refund from a vendor who didn't notify me they would be charging me again, even though I was close to saying "yes" to the renewal. Don't be that person. It's just rude.

INCENTIVES FOR QUICK PAYMENT

While this isn't really a financing term, per se, it's an important item to consider. Some people need a bit of a boost to sign on the dotted line. A couple of great ways to accomplish this are a guarantee (more about that in a sec) or an incentive for signing up right away.

Incentives you could consider include offering an additional resource (like a book or set of worksheets), an additional coaching session, or something else of value.

MONEY-BACK GUARANTEES

I typically only offer money-back guarantees with my direct to consumer services (like coaching and workshops). I find that offering them eliminates a risk factor for potential clients (Will I like it? Is it worth it?), which makes it easier for them to make the decision to purchase. Yes!

People rarely ask for their money back, especially when you're fulfilling the promises your marketing copy makes. And besides, you can avoid a ton of bad will from an unhappy customer by refunding their money.

When offering a guarantee, I'd recommend that you choose a timeframe (like 30, 60, or 90 days) that allows your customer just enough time to experience your services, but not so much that they get the complete benefit from working with you.

PAYMENT METHODS

Credit cards

Lots of people ask me how to charge clients for their credit card processing fees (like you have when using Stripe or Square in order to accept credit card payments).

You don't. It's a cost of doing business.

So build it into the cost of your service, and if you get paid in a way that doesn't incur the same fees, it's just a little bonus for you.

And remember, too, with credit card purchases, you're typically getting paid right away (or within a couple of days), instead of having to wait for an invoice to be paid. There's value in that. Credit cards also make it easier for your clients to say "yes," which is worth something to you and your business, too.

Bank transfers/ACH

Most of my corporate clients pay me through invoice and bank transfer, which works great. (ACH is Automated Clearing House, which is a network that facilitates electronic payments.)

When I have large consulting agreements, bank transfers work especially well. I don't have to wait for a check to be mailed, or worry about it getting lost in transit (or remembering to deposit it), and it's great to not to have to pay credit card fees on large invoices.

One way to save time and look professional to your client is to have a couple of documents at the ready. First is a W-9 form (it's a form for US taxes that shows your taxpayer ID number, or social security number if you don't have a TIN/EIN). Just print one out, add your info, sign it, and scan it so it's ready when you need it.

The second form is one you'll create yourself with your bank deposit information. I split mine into two sections: Payee Information (that's me) and Bank Information (that's my bank). Payee Information includes the name on the bank account, contact name, contact phone, and email address. The Bank Information section has the bank name, ABA routing number, account number, type of account, and account classification (mine is a business account).

If you have both of these forms ready to go, it makes it even easier for your client to get you into their system and get paid. Fast.

Other methods

I still have a couple of corporate clients who pay by check, which works fine. It's just not as seamless for me as a direct deposit. For individual clients, though, I don't accept checks. I don't want to deal with them, although I know some folks who are perfectly fine with getting paid by check.

Other methods of getting paid, like PayPal, Venmo, and Zelle, can be effective if they work for both you and your client.

Payment methods, like all customer-facing systems, make impressions of their own, though, so think about the image you want to portray to your clients. And be sure you follow the terms of any payment service; some don't allow business transactions without a business account.

SLOW PAY/NO PAY

What do you do when your client is either slow to pay or simply doesn't pay at all?

Be sure to address the slow pay issue in your payment terms. It's common practice to have fees for late payment (or discounts for fast payment, which amounts to pretty much the same thing). Make it in the customer's best interest to pay you on time…or even early. It's much easier to deal with a client who's slow to pay when you know you'll be collecting some extra fees for it.

If you have a policy of requiring up-front payments (or a significant deposit up front), it's important to keep your boundaries clear: don't start work until you've received your initial payment. It's tempting to jump right in, but in the spirit of teaching your client how to treat you, they need to know that you stick with your agreements (and you don't work for free).

The same holds true if the client is late with agreed-upon payments later in the agreement. I do like to give a little leeway for first-time lateness, but it's certainly okay to tell the client that you need to pause work while things get sorted on the finance front. Give them notice (let them know there's a balance outstanding) and opportunity (to make things right).

When a client doesn't pay — at all — that's a whole new issue to contend with. My first recommendation is to go back to the agreement. What terms did you both agree to? (And you *do* have a signed agreement, right?) If there's a signed agreement, let it be the focus, not you or them. That can be a big help in preserving your relationships.

You can say, "According to our agreement, there is a $5,000 up-front fee before we start working together. I haven't received it yet. How do you recommend we resolve this?"

Sometimes, corporate clients aren't aware of what's going on in the finance or procurement side of the house, and they may not realize you haven't yet been paid. Because they're motivated to move the project forward, clients can be great allies inside the company to cut through any red tape.

With individual clients, it can be a bit tougher to resolve, since they're the both the customer and the person who makes the payments happen. Be firm (although you can be kind at the same time).

In the event that you've completed work for a client and you have an outstanding balance that they're not paying, you may need to take other measures. Be sure you've done the whole notice and opportunity piece first, but if they still don't pay, you may need to talk with your attorney to enforce the terms of your contract.

PRO TIPS

- Pay particular attention to payment terms — they can have a big impact on your business.
- Ask your individual clients to pay you up front for all but the largest packages, and ask your corporate clients to make a significant up-front investment. They help you, and they also help your client.
- Incentives for quick payment and money-back guarantees can help make it easier for clients to say "yes" to your services.
- Bake any credit card fees into your pricing — it's a cost of doing business.
- Don't work for free; wait for your payment before starting work on the engagement.
- If your client is slow to pay (or won't pay), focus on your agreement with them to get things back on track. And get advice from your attorney if you can't make things work.

Chapter 14

To Negotiate or Not to Negotiate

A big part of the work I do in my practice is coaching clients how to negotiate your pay package. I even wrote a book about it (**Pay Up!** *Unlocking Insider Secrets of Salary Negotiation*). So I'm a major fan of negotiating, in general.

The big thing that's different about salary negotiation and pricing negotiation is that salary negotiation starts with the *employer's* offer, and pricing typically starts from *your offer*. So I guess you could say that I support negotiating theirs, but not so much yours.

WHEN (AND HOW) TO NEGOTIATE

There are a couple of places I'd recommend getting your negotiation on:

Temporary assignments. The employer will likely have a stated rate or range, and you may be able to negotiate upwards based on your qualifications, the rarity of your skills, plus other factors (like a red-hot job market or the employer's urgency to fill the role).

Freelance agreement rates. This is a bit of a "maybe." I recommend that you set your rate and stick to it; however, if a company is willing to offer more hours and/or a longer engagement, you could offer a small discount in consideration (see Chapter 10).

Freelance and consulting agreement terms. Some of your terms can be negotiated. And when you're negotiating with corporate clients, you may find that you need to be flexible to come to an agreement that works for you both. Items like financing terms, insurance, and indemnity clauses may have boilerplate language from the company that they insist on including.

When negotiating with corporate clients, you may find that you need to be flexible to come to an agreement that works for you both.

I always (always!) recommend that you run any agreement by your attorney before signing, especially when the organization says "it's standard," or "we always do it like this." Issues like intellectual property and sales rights will always be written in favor of the company, and you don't want to inadvertently sign your important rights away.

WHEN TO SKIP THE NEGOTIATIONS

In most of the cases included in this book, I'd recommend skipping the negotiation piece. Clients may want to negotiate with you, but it's a slippery slope, and with all the moving parts to your services, it's hard to negotiate on the fly. They don't know what you do or what it takes to do it. If you're firm — but pleasant — when declining to negotiate, you're teaching your clients how to treat you.

WHAT TO DO INSTEAD

So…if you can't negotiate, what *can* you do? There are several ways to serve your clients without negotiating your rates downward.

Reduce services. If an organization lets you know that they're not able to afford your consulting proposal, it's smart to have a plan. I always recommend pulling products or services out of the proposal (with a corresponding fee decrease) rather than reducing the fees to complete the entire proposal.

And there are a few ways to do that. You could remove specific deliverables, or you could reduce the complexity (and time spent) on the deliverables. Or, you might consider breaking the proposal into phases, and tackling them one at a time so the client is only investing a smaller amount up front. The client can then make choices to add deliverables, details, or phases back in at a later date.

Down-sell. If a client is reluctant to make an investment with you, it's always great to have some sort of way they can connect with your messaging or experience you in a different way. This works best with selling to individuals rather than organizations.

For example, if a potential client isn't a great fit for my individual salary negotiation coaching services, I have a self-paced online class that's far less expensive. I also have a book on the topic (less expensive still), and I've written multiple articles and blog posts, which are available on my website (free).

Refer. Sometimes, clients come to us for services we *could* provide, but we might not be the exact right choice. For example, I have a friend who's a career transition coach, and sometimes her clients want her to help them with resume writing. She refers those clients to other consultants — it winds up being less costly for the client, and she doesn't get bogged down in work she doesn't love doing.

It's always smart to help your client find a solution that works, whether or not that includes negotiation!

PRO TIPS

- Negotiating your rates works best for temporary assignments and sometimes with freelance rates.
- Consider which of your freelance or consulting terms you would be willing to negotiate.
- If a client wants to negotiate your fees or pricing, consider reducing services, down-selling, or referring a client instead.

Chapter 15

The Sales Conversation

O kay, let me say straight up that sales is not my specialty. In fact, just writing this chapter makes me uncomfortable. Which, frankly, is a lot like the sales conversation itself: scary, uncomfortable, but it's got to be done!

Here's a collection of my best advice on the selling process.

KNOW, LIKE, AND TRUST

The adage that we buy from people we know, like, and trust is the real deal. It's a rare thing for people to buy from or select someone they've never heard of.

When you really focus on helping the client get to a decision — whether that's yes *or* no — your perspective will automatically orient you to a service mindset.

That's why having a presence on whatever social media channels your clients hang out on is important. If you've got a website with examples of your work or articles you've written about the topic you freelance or consult on, so much the better. And make sure whatever you write or say sounds authentically like you, not some automaton. That authenticity helps with the trust factor.

Think of this thought leadership work as a critical part of your sales process, and it'll feel a lot less onerous, I promise!

HOW CLIENTS MAKE PURCHASE DECISIONS

Did you know that people make decisions emotionally, and use facts to reinforce the decisions they've already made? It's true!

As much as people want you to think they evaluate everything logically, that step largely happens after the emotional decision has happened. Harvard Business School professor Gerald Zaltman's consumer research shows that the great majority (95%!) of our purchasing decisions are made subconsciously.

All that work you did in Chapter 2 around your value proposition will come into play in your sales conversation. Connect with what your client values and what they stand for, and you'll be connecting with them on a gut level. Then the sales conversation will become far easier.

DON'T FOCUS ON CLOSING THE SALE

A lot of people say that the goal of every sales call is to make the sale, and if you can't get them to say "yes," you absolutely *don't* want them to say "no." I disagree.

My position is that in any sales conversation, your goal should be to help your potential client *reach a decision*. It should not be focused on convincing them to say "yes." When you're driving towards "yes," it's really easy to shift into what I call "grabby energy," where you're chasing the sale. And face it, we've all been on the receiving end of grabby energy (think of the used car salesman trope) — it feels super-gross. Don't do that.

When you really focus on helping the client get to a decision — whether that's yes *or* no — your perspective will automatically orient you to a service mindset. Which likely gets to the heart of why you're in a service-oriented business in the first place. That approach doesn't feel grabby or gross at all.

Your clients will be better served by making a decision to opt in or opt out than they will by not making a choice. For corporate clients, you may have to go back and forth to refine their problem statement before they can agree to a proposal — and that is absolutely fine. You want them to be clear before starting your work together.

With individual clients, there's typically not the same back-and-forth process. If they have trouble making a decision, ask them what's standing in their way. Many times, they'll say it's money (or they need to check with their spouse about it). Why is that? What needs to be true for them to make a decision?

If your services require significant investment, it's natural for clients to need a day or two to consider. But don't let things go unresolved. If they need a day to consider, take a moment *in that meeting* to schedule a follow up call. And then ask them for a decision — either way — on that call.

Not every client will (or should, frankly) say "yes." And when it's okay with you either way the decision goes, you'll show up calmer and more relaxed and in service for your client. We'll talk more about emotional distance later in the book (Chapter 18), but moving away from "I gotta close the sale!" is a great example of it.

SELLING TO PAST CLIENTS RATHER THAN NEW ONES

Selling services to past (or current) clients is almost always easier than selling services to a new client. You've established a relationship with them, you know more about them, and they have experienced the great results they get when they work with you.

Of course, some businesses offer more of the one-and-done-type services, but if yours isn't one of them, think about how you might design services you can sell to folks you've already worked with.

You can certainly sell to new clients every time, but if you can make the sales process easier for yourself, why wouldn't you?

THE "ADDED EXTRAS" APPROACH

I like to be proactive with my clients throughout our time together, and selling consulting proposals is no exception. Part of the work I do to prepare my proposal is to listen closely as the client describes the issues they would like help solving.

While that's the main focus of the proposal, I often have ideas for extra services that would serve the client well. I'll include these additional services in the proposal for the client to consider along with the services that address the original ask. And many times, clients add these services (and their extra fees) to our agreements.

There are tons of great books about sales and selling, so if this is an area of focus for you, I recommend picking up one or more of them (check out the Resource Reference Guide for suggestions).

PRO TIPS

- Selling can feel uncomfortable, but you must master the process if you want to have a successful business.
- People make sales decisions emotionally, and then use facts to justify those gut decisions. Connect with clients' hearts and their heads.
- Focus on helping your client reach a decision, not on closing the sale. You'll shift more authentically into service mode and away from grabby energy.
- Current or former clients are easier to sell to than new ones.
- Consider proposing additional services to your clients — they might just take you up on them.

Chapter 16

What to Say...and What NOT to

S ales, pricing, and terms conversations are hard. And when you don't know what to say, they can be super-duper-extra-hard. So here are some sample scripts for you to try — and tailor for your business — for some of the most common situations that come up in this space.

PRICE INCREASES

If you're in business for any length of time, price increases will become a regular part of your business operations. This is an important skill to master.

Don't say this...

> "I'm really sorry to have to tell you, but I feel like I really have to increase my pricing. But if you can't pay that much, it's totally okay."

So much wrong! Let's break it down.

Do not apologize. Don't. This is a business transaction; it isn't personal. And you have nothing to apologize for, for heaven's sake!

Don't use wishy-washy words. It's time to jettison words like "think," "feel," and "believe," from your business vocabulary. Especially when you're negotiating or having a discussion around pricing or terms.

Don't negate yourself. If there's a pricing increase, there's a pricing increase. If there isn't; there isn't. Don't put it out there if you're not serious about it. There are ways to transition your current clients into new pricing (more in Chapter 12); you're welcome to use those ideas if they would benefit you and/or your business.

Say this instead:

> "I wanted to let you know that my prices will be increasing at the beginning of <month/year>."

No apologies, wishy-washy language, or equivocation. Straight to the point. See how much better that sounds?

If you want to create a renewal incentive like we discussed in Chapter 13, try this (I'll add in some sample months so you can get the hang of it):

> "I wanted to let you know that my prices will be increasing at the beginning of January. Since your agreement ends in December, as a valued client, I would be happy to extend your current pricing through March if you renew next year's annual agreement by the end of November. The new pricing would take effect in April."

This approach offers your client an incentive (three months at the old pricing) in exchange for signing next year's contract before you would typically sign in January. And while you don't benefit from higher prices for the entire year (only nine months of it), your client will be paying a higher average price over the course of the year.

DISCOUNTS

Be up front about any discounts you're offering to your client. I always put them into my proposals and agreements, and it's also something I highlight with my clients about when we're discussing the documents.

Don't use wishy-washy language.

There are a couple of reasons for this. First, it's important to anchor your clients to your real rates, which reflect your value. Just because the price has been discounted doesn't mean that your value is less. Your clients need to know that for their own purposes, and it's also crucial they're aware they're getting special pricing when they refer you to others.

And secondly, if you decide to change your practices around which clients are offered pro bono, low-bono, or otherwise discounted rates down the road, it will be more apparent to your clients that it's the discount that's changing, not the actual rate.

Don't say this...

<Nothing; your client knows they're getting a deal!>

Say this instead:

"I'm pleased to offer you an X% discount off my normal rates for the term of this engagement to reflect <reasons>."

Again, make sure you're telling them about their awesome and special pricing.

PREMIUMS

Rush or last-minute services are of value, and when you don't charge for them, you're basically telling your clients that your schedule is of no consequence. And even if a rush job doesn't cause you to pull an all-nighter, or delay work for another client *this* time, there's a very good chance that it could in the future.

Rush fees are a cost of doing business at the last minute. And most clients are aware of it. If you're not charging a premium above your regular rates for rush service, think about why it doesn't make sense for you.

If your client asks you to complete a deliverable with a turnaround time that's much faster than usual, be up front about it.

Don't say this...

> "Sure, I'll fit this in, no problem." <Nervously bites nails and curses to self.>

Don't give up your pricing power to be nice. Sure, it's important to be pleasant and polite in any business conversation, but if a client wants something above and beyond what's laid out in your agreement, they should pay for it. Saying it loud for the folks in the back.

Say this instead:

> "I can definitely fit your important project into my schedule. Because your expected turnaround of 24 hours is considerably quicker than my normal seven-day delivery window, there will be a X% rush charge applied to the deliverable, which will bring your cost to $Y. That's how we've laid out rush charges in the contract, and I just wanted to highlight it to you and get your okay to move forward."

Do get the rush charge okayed. If it's a normal part of your business, I encourage you to add a section to your freelance agreement (I still like to highlight to clients when it comes into play). If it's not a typical charge, it's even more important to spell it out —and get agreement from the client in writing beforehand.

You can use this method for just about any type of premium you need to implement mid-engagement. Most premiums won't be visible to your clients, since you'll build them into their initial pricing.

BOUNDARIES

In the spirit of teaching your clients how to treat you (more in Chapter 7), you must create boundaries for yourself and your business. Otherwise, your clients will do it for you, which may or may not reflect practices you want to adopt.

When your client asks you to complete additional work. Additional work can be awesome! I think of it a bit like remodeling — once your expert contractor gets on site, you're reminded of all sorts of additional things they could help you with. And just like contractors do, you need to charge for your extra work.

Don't say this...

> "Sure, we'll fit that in. Somehow. Not sure how, but yeah."

Say this instead:

> "That sure sounds like an interesting project, and I'd love to talk more about it. Since it's outside of the scope of our original agreement, we'll need to put together an addendum with the deliverables and fees. Would you like me to run up a draft for you?"

When your client asks you to begin work before you've received your up-front payment. It can be so tempting to start working on a new engagement that it's easy to ignore all the terms you spent time creating. But don't.

Don't say this...

"Yay! Let's dive in right away! Can't wait!"

Say this instead:

"I'm eager to get started on your ultra-cool project! We can begin work as soon as we have all the signed agreements completed, and I've received the up-front payment we discussed. Looking forward to it!"

When your client's payment is late. If your client is slow to pay their invoices, the worst thing you can do is to say nothing. Letting things slide teaches your client that it's okay to drag their feet.

Don't say this...

<Nothing. Ignoring the issue. Nervously.>

Say this instead:

"I wanted to let you know that I haven't yet received the payment that was due on XX date. Could you please check with your finance team and let me know when to expect it? I would hate for this to impact our timeline, but if the payment isn't here by the end of the week, we'll need to put things on hold until it gets here."

When your client doesn't provide timely feedback. Sometimes, clients are slow to provide feedback or edits, which can hold up the project and work.

Don't say this...

"Wow, I'm going to have to pull an all-nighter and miss my kid's birthday party in order to meet our deadline since you waited until twelve hours before the deadline to provide feedback. That makes me very sad and mad."

Say this instead:

"Our service agreement says I'll have 48 hours to turn around the final design once all feedback is submitted. I received the latest updates at 8 p.m., so I'll deliver your final files no later than 8 p.m. on <two days from today>."

This is another example of using your agreement as the focus, rather than the client themselves.

PRO TIPS

- Don't shy away from tough conversations because you don't know what to say. Try these scripts, and change them around for your own business.
- Don't apologize, use wishy-washy words, or negate yourself when you're talking with clients about pricing.
- Make sure your client knows it when they're receiving a discount.
- It's fine to charge premiums for your work, especially for things like rush service. Build them into your agreements, and stick to them in practice.
- Create healthy boundaries with your clients so you can serve them well.

Chapter 17
Skillset Q&A

Q: What time of the year is best for raising prices?
A: You can raise your prices any time! That said, many of my clients find it easier to use the beginning of a calendar year to set their new rates.

Q: I just got my business certified as a B Corp, and want to offer a discount to other B Corps. How can I justify that to my other clients?
A: Go, B Corps (or Benefit Corporations, for the uninitiated — see bcorporation.net for more info)! It's perfectly fine to offer discounts to certain clients and not to others. I offer discounts to nonprofits and B Corps myself. Be clear – in writing – that you're offering them a discount to your regular prices (and why you're doing it). No need to justify or discuss it with your other clients.

Q: I haven't raised my prices in 5 years, but I'm in the middle of a certification program right now. I should wait until I get my certification to raise my rates, right?
A: Nope! If you haven't touched your prices in that long, you probably need to raise them right now. And if you find that your certification commands higher prices in the market, you can raise your rates again once you get it!

Q: What can I do so I don't have to chase my client around every month to get them to pay me?
A: The easiest way to solve this is to have them pay you up front for your services. If there are any ways to make it easier for your client to automatically pay you (auto-bill a credit card or some other sort of e-pay), try that. You can

also add a term into your contracts that specifies late fees, and follow up with your updated invoices (plus your late fees!) on the regular.

Q: How do I charge my clients for the credit card fees I have? Is it better to use something like Venmo that doesn't charge me a fee?
A: Build the cost of the fees into your pricing. Your client doesn't need to know (or care) about what it costs you to run your business.

Whatever you do, make it easy for your client. If they like to pay by credit card, by all means offer that to them.

Also, if you use a payment service, be sure you're permitted to use it for business. Many apps don't allow it (or require a business account with different terms).

Q: Can I just skip some of the financing terms? I want the client to know I trust them.
A: There's a difference between trusting your clients and sharing your expectations with them. My experience is that clients aren't put off by seeing cancellation policies and how quickly they need to pay. It's business, after all. But skip them at your own peril. Not having a signed agreement with the terms you need is a recipe for disaster.

Q: My client wants to negotiate the pricing of the consulting proposal I just sent out. Help!
A: The best advice here is to negotiate the deliverables rather than the overall pricing. Think of your proposal like an outfit of shirt, pants, socks, shoes, and accessories. Instead of discounting the entire outfit, negotiate for one (or more) of the items to be excluded. That way, if the client wants to have the complete outfit, they can add the pre-

viously excluded item back in, and you haven't discounted your prices.

Q: Am I a jerk for not starting work until I get paid? Our agreement said I'd get paid up front, and while they still haven't come up with the check, my client is pressuring me to get started.
A: No. It's important to keep your boundaries, which also means keeping to the terms of your agreement. Having a "pay up front" policy helps you put pressure on your client to do the right thing — if they can't get any deliverables completed, they'll prioritize payment.

Just lean on your agreement ("I'm really eager to get started on this interesting project! Since our agreement calls for payment up front, all I'll need from you all is the check, and we'll be able to move forward.").

Q: Help! The client wants rush service, but I'm worried they won't want to pay the extra charges in our contract.
A: Let your contract be your friend — you put those terms in for a reason (and the client signed on). Just be up front about it. Let them know the turnaround time will fall into the rush pricing category indicated in the contract, and that you just wanted them to be aware that they'll see the additional charge on their invoice.

Q: My Fortune 500 client is SO SLOW paying my invoices, but I'm just a small fish for them. It's infuriating. Is there anything I can do?
A: I feel for you! I've been in this situation — it's no fun to chase after money you've already earned. There are a couple of things I'd recommend in this situation. First, make sure your agreement with them spells out how fast they need to pay. If their 90-day (or whatever it is) payment period

is part of the contract and you don't like it, you're out of luck…at least for this agreement.

Be sure to change things up in your contract next time. If they're not keeping to the terms of your agreement, call their billing department and see what you can do to get things back on track, and be sure to let your client know that there's an issue with billing that could impact your ability to complete your deliverables. Worst case is that you stop work with the client while they get current with their payments.

PART 3

MINDSET

We've talked about:

…Your Toolset — the tools and information you need to make great decisions

…Your Skillset — the skills you need to get it done

Now, let's talk about your Mindset. This section will help you set your intention for establishing your pricing and terms (plus any conversations you have with clients) and get out of your own way.

What's in this section…

Chapter 18: It's Not Personal

How our socialization tricks us. Selling services, not personal worth. Seeing pricing as a business transaction. Credentials, value, and pricing. The importance of market positioning and emotional distancing

Chapter 19: Mindset Shifts

Why rejecting assumptions about yourself and your client serves you well. Seven types of mindset shifts to adopt. Deciding how you want to show up for your clients.

Chapter 20: Why You Hesitate

The four most common reasons freelancers and consultants hesitate (perfection, permission, discovery, and confidence), and how to tackle them.

Chapter 21: Managing Your Energy

Thinking about yourself as the product with service businesses.
Selling your energy. Preserving your energy, and what happens
when you don't. How to recharge.

Chapter 22: Mindset Q&A

Questions I get about topics in the Mindset section (and how I
answer them).

Chapter 18
It's Not Personal

Pricing your services and naming your terms feels personal, but it really isn't. And taking things personally can trip you up in how you think, plan, and talk about terms and pricing.

It's *your* business, so why isn't it this personal?

IT'S A BUSINESS TRANSACTION

While the work you do with your clients may have components that aren't within the traditional realm of business (like intuition, emotion, energy, or whatever it may be), the actual sale of your work, the pricing of your services, and the terms under which you do all of it should be considered business transactions. *Because they are.*

And business transactions are not personal. They can *feel* personal, but they're really not. And it's important to remember that as you enter into agreements with your clients.

IT'S A SOCIAL THING

Many of us have been socialized to think we're less worthy than others are. That's simply not true.

For any member of a historically marginalized group (people of color, women, LBGTQIA+, differently abled, or others), it's almost universally true that they've been told — more often than not, directly and multiple times — that they're not worth as much as those in power.

And to top it all off, there's the family conditioning, messages from schools and jobs and sports, media reinforcement, and, and, and... It can feel overwhelming.

So there's history to overcome here. And it won't be easy. But don't define your own worth by someone else's standards.

YOUR PRICE IS NOT YOUR WORTH

What your client pays for your services says a whole lot more about how they value the services you provide than about your worth as a person. You'll run into people who don't think you should charge what you do, and that's because they do not value the service.

You'll likely also have clients who think the work you do together is worth more than they've paid (although they may not be quite as likely to tell you so, for obvious reasons).

When you provide services to your clients, it's not about you. *It's all about your clients.*

Even when you get paid gigantic buckets of cash for what you do, it's *still* not a reflection of your worth. What a client pays you is a reflection of the worth of your services. *To them.*

Say it with me: "My pricing is not a reflection of my value or worth as a human being."

When you can put it into the perspective of the value you're providing to your clients, it becomes more of an economics discussion than a self-worth one. Getting a bit of emotional distance will help you get the proper perspective on this work.

IT'S NOT ABOUT YOU, ANYWAY

When you provide services to your clients, it's not about you. *It's all about your clients.*

Your business is all about providing value to them (and remember, they determine the value). Your customers *should* be focused on the work you're doing together and the results they're getting. You don't want them thinking about your agenda and what's going on with you.

When someone doesn't make the "buy" decision, or if they decide not to extend a contract, that's not about you. It's about the client. When a prospective client doesn't like your pricing, that says a lot more about them than about you, too. And when you can't come to terms with a client, it just means that you and they aren't a good match. Again, not about you.

On the flip side of the coin, the same is true: even the good things are not about you. Which blows some people's minds, but it shouldn't. When a client loves your services, or has a huge success when working with you, that's not about you, either. Oh, it is so, so ego-boosting to think it might be, but it's not.

GET SOME EMOTIONAL DISTANCE

One of the best ways you can make the right choices for your business and to have meaningful conversations with your clients is to get a bit of emotional distance from the whole thing.

Think about how you might approach these conversations if you were pricing or selling a friend's services. You're not completely obsessed with making a sale or convincing the client to accept your terms, right? You're just concentrating on the business transaction. That's the ticket!

The "not about you" mantra helps give you a bit of distance (especially when you can apply it to the good stuff as well as the bad).

What does this emotional distance provide? It gives you more freedom to do your best work. Which is important when you're selling or establishing your pricing or terms. All of that emotionally trigger-y stuff takes up a ton of processing space in your brain that you could be putting to better use. Like listening to your client and showing up the way you want to.

PRO TIPS

- The work you do in the sales, terms, and pricing space is all about the business transactions. It's not personal.
- What a client is willing to pay for your services reflects how valuable your services are to them, not a reflection of your worth. It's not personal.
- Our feelings of worth (and/or lack thereof) are socialized into us from an early age, so feelings can run deep. It is not personal.
- When you can create some emotional distance between you and your work, you're more likely to have successful conversations with your clients. Because...it's not personal.

Chapter 19
Mindset Shifts

A ny conversations you have with your clients around pricing, terms, or sales can be challenging. You can make things way easier for yourself with the right mindset.

REJECT ASSUMPTIONS

In any pricing or terms discussion, it's crucial that you get rid of any negative assumptions you have about your potential/current client and yourself.

I've had dozens of conversations about pricing with folks that begin with, "I know I should charge more, but my client can't afford it." Really? You've checked their bank account? You know their long-term financial picture? Do. Not. Do. This.

Price things the way your research and design process tells you to price them. Not to pretzel your pricing into a space you imagine your clients would like/accept/not freak out about.

I've had nonprofit consulting clients who have invested more with me than Fortune 100 clients did, and recent college graduates who spent more than executives. You can't fully know the motivations and decision points your clients have.

Don't make negative assumptions about yourself, either. Some call these "limiting beliefs," and whatever you call them, they're not helpful, especially in pricing conversations. We're talking anything from "I stink at pricing," to "I'm not worth that much," (see Chapter 18), to "Why would they listen to little old me?" Get rid of the negative self-talk.

One of the best prep steps you can take is to write down all the assumptions you have about yourself and your client, and really take a look at them. Which ones don't serve the conversation or communication you'll be having with your client?

When you're ready to shift your mindset about them, do yourself a favor. Make up three additional stories about what might be true instead of the assumption you made. And then, intentionally let go of anything in your original assumption list or your additional stories list that won't help you.

RESET YOUR MINDSET

There are seven basic mindset shifts that can serve you as you approach pricing and sales conversations.

From Scarcity to Abundance. This is a biggie. When your focus is on limitations and protecting what you have, it's really tough to be open to important inputs, like what your client needs and what is happening around you.

From Waiting to Progress. We'll cover this more extensively in Chapter 20, but bottom line, stop waiting for whatever you're waiting for, and get it done!

From Security to Opportunity. Security can feel lovely and safe, but just like with playground play structures, you absolutely must let go (at least with one hand!) in order to grasp the opportunity that's in front of you.

From Saving to Investment. One of the most challenging mindset shifts for new business owners can be moving from saving to spending. I don't mean spending for spending's sake, but investing in the tools and resources you need to do business.

Don't skip working with experts in service of saving money. And don't avoid using tools like credit card processing or an invoicing system because they cost money. Investing in your business is part of your job.

From All the Options to Opting In. It can seem like abundance to have all of the choices available instead of choosing just one, but it's actually not, for two reasons. First is mindspace. When you have tons of options (like the types of clients you'll serve or services you'll offer), each one takes up a little bit — or a lot — of brain-processing space. You already have enough on your mind, don't you?

Second is actually making a choice and doing something. As long as your options are all floating around, you don't actually have to commit to anything, and if you're not committing, you can't dig in and go deep.

From Fear to Possibility. Oh, yes, my friend! I realize this work can be scary. Really scary, even. But when you dwell on the fear instead of what could be possible, you can freeze yourself into inaction. You know what's on the other side of your fear, once you walk through it? Possibility. *That's* exciting.

From Competition to Collaboration. Instead of thinking about your client as a competitor (e.g. the only way for you to win is for them to lose), try imagining them as collaborators. After all, pricing and agreements are business opportunities, and an agreement isn't only for one of the two parties.

KNOW HOW YOU WANT TO SHOW UP

After you reject assumptions and reset your mindset, it's time to get intentional about how you want to show up for your current or potential clients.

Every interaction you have with a potential client shows them what it's like to work with you. Take a sec and read that again. Every single one. And your proposal and selling process can be some of your best opportunities to make a great impression.

Exactly what kind of impression do you want to make on your clients? What would you like them to notice about you? (I don't mean this hypothetically — do take a moment and answer these questions for yourself.)

If you want clients to think you're easy to work with, make sure your systems and processes are set up to eliminate speed bumps for your clients. If clients should know you're professional, think about how you can show that to them. If you want to be known as responsive, how will that show up (and what will your boundaries be)?

Here are some of the top things that can impact how you're perceived:

Preparation. When you're meeting a client, they need to know you have your head in the game. Even if they don't. Take time to fully prepare every time you meet a client — and especially for any proposal, selling, or pricing conversation. And while I personally hate rescheduling, if you're not ready to meet a client, it's better to meet at a different time when you *are* prepared.

This sounds so simple, but it's not. Your thorough preparation is fundamental to any service-oriented business. If you find yourself so busy that it's hard to prepare in advance of your client meetings, that can be a great indication that you need to raise your prices and drop some clients.

The customer *isn't* always right.

Confidence. With service businesses, you're typically selling your expertise. One of the ways clients assess your expertise — right or wrong — is through your confidence. Which can sometimes be a bit of a challenge.

There are ways to manufacture a bit of confidence, especially as it relates to your skills, knowledge, and expertise. One exercise I recommend is an extension of the work we talked about in defining your ideal client (Chapter 2). Write down fifty things that you know or can do that your ideal client doesn't know or can't do.

Once you get rooted in your own expertise, it's easier to project confidence. And eliminate wishy-washy language from your vocabulary (Chapter 16) — that helps a ton, too!

Timeliness. From conference calls to service delivery, your clients want to know they can count on you to be on time. It's a professional courtesy that means more to some clients than others, but it's never wrong to be timely.

One of the places people miss when they think of timeliness? Billing. Bill your clients on time. I mean it. Even if you have to outsource your invoicing in order to get it done. Timely billing is critically important for your own bottom line (yay, solvency!), but it's also a key way to show you're a real businessperson who takes their business seriously. When you bill your clients on time, they'll be much more likely to pay you in a timely fashion. And the reverse is true, too.

Systems and processes. I'm not a systems-y or process-y person. That work doesn't come naturally to me. But I am absolutely a stickler about it. I love systems and processes, because once they're set up, I don't have to deal with them again. At least not for a long time. But I truly do care about them, because a) they make things easier for my clients, b) they make my work life simpler and more streamlined, and c) they show my clients that I'm serious about my business.

Don't leave it to chance. And don't ignore how you show up because you want to be authentic. Being intentional doesn't mean pretending, and being off the cuff doesn't automatically make you authentic.

What about "the customer is always right"? I kinda don't love this phrase. Yes, you absolutely should be responsive and pleasant to all of your clients, and it's vitally important that you know them well. But there are many times where you, as the expert, will know more about what the client needs than they might. And there are situations where clients don't behave well, too. So…in my book, not always right.

In service businesses, focusing on collaboration with the client works a whole lot better than slavish dedication to satisfying even the most unreasonable client requests. You have standards, processes, methods, and business practices that you've spent lots of time developing. Don't toss them out the window for a client just so they will think you're "nice." (News flash: they'll just think you're a pushover anyway.)

PRO TIPS

- Making assumptions about your client or yourself can torpedo your sales and pricing conversations. Kick them to the curb (your assumptions, not your clients)!
- If you find yourself getting anxious about a sales or pricing conversation, reset your mindset.
- Be intentional about how you show up for your clients with your preparation, confidence, timeliness, and processes.
- The customer *isn't* always right.

Chapter 20
Why You Hesitate

To be honest, there are a million reasons people hesitate to raise their prices, have difficult conversations about agreement terms, put a new service offering out there, or just about anything that's challenging in their business.

But most of the reasons we stay stuck and don't take actions can be narrowed down into one of four categories:

1. **Perfection.** "I must be certain it's right."
2. **Permission:** "Someone must tell me it's okay."
3. **Discovery:** "Someone will find me or rescue me."
4. **Confidence:** "I need to have confidence in order to proceed."

PERFECTION

This is a biggie for many of my clients, and it's probably the one I get hung up on most, myself. A lot of this hesitation stems from the belief that, since we are the product, anything that represents us needs to be perfect. Or that we need to wait for the exactly right moment to act.

Not true.

In fact, you can use your imperfection as part of your strategy. For instance, I know an author who (after careful editing and proofreading) invites her readers to report any typos in the published book to her, and rewards them with book-related swag.

And many course creators (including me!) offer special pricing when they hold the course for the first time, and invite attendees to provide feedback to shape the next round. It can be freeing to be up front with your clients and to engage them in the process.

When we wait until something is exactly, perfectly, correct, there's a great chance it won't ever get out there or get done. There's always something else to tweak or play with or procrastinate over…you get the picture.

You're the first, best advocate for you and your business.

While it is smart to be aware of timing, you're not likely to be able to time everything perfectly. And waiting until it's the exact right time for your client (like lining up your price increase up with your client's budgeting cycle) may mean you miss out on revenue for yourself.

I had a truly exceptional client who struggled in this space — smart as a whip and kind as the day is long. Her consulting clients *love* her. But she would obsess about details to the point of not sending things out.

We looked at her long relationship with perfectionism, and in the end, she had to create different standards for herself. One thing that helped? The notion that a grade of 90% is an "A" in most places.

Does this mean you can be slapdash and put anything in front of your client? Absolutely not. But don't struggle so hard for that last little bit of perfection. If you've nailed your 90%, chances are good that your client won't notice (or care) about the rest.

P.S. Done is better than perfect. It's never, ever going to be perfect. And that's okay.

PERMISSION

Tons of people get hung up on waiting for permission before they act. And many times, they're seeking that permission from the client. Trust me, it's a rare thing for a client to let you know that it's time to raise your prices or ask for a contract renewal.

It's your business. You must take charge. Just like you teach your clients how to treat you, you're also the expert in the services you provide and the business you run. You're the first, best advocate for you and your business. That means taking risks, making mistakes, and most importantly, learning from your risks and mistakes.

What we're talking about here is essentially the difference between being proactive and reactive. Proactive folks take initiative; reactive folks respond to others taking initiative. You don't want someone else setting your agenda, especially around pricing.

If you've never heard this before, let me be the first: *you don't need permission.* There.

DISCOVERY

For women and people of color, some of this "waiting for discovery" may be wrapped up in the socialization of, "If I do a really, really good job, people will notice me, pick me, and reward me." Blech. But hey, I got this drilled into me, too, and it's hard to break free from.

With freelancers and consultants, it's simply not enough to do great work and be done with it. While that perspective is likely to be a bit more successful if you're working for someone else, it's not a great tactic even then. And when you're on your own, it's a recipe for disaster.

It's your responsibility to attract clients to your business (scary, but true). There are dozens of ways you can make it easier for clients to find you, some of which work better for certain types of services. But here are four main avenues.

Thought leadership. If you're selling your expertise as a service, thought leadership is pretty much non-negotiable. It's also not quick. Much of thought leadership revolves around creating content like books, articles, blogs, podcast appearances, speaking engagements, training courses, videos, and social media.

It can seem daunting, but most content can be repurposed across channels, in some way or another.

Referrals. My favorite source of referrals is former clients. They know what it's like to work with me, and chances are good that potential clients will get a realistic preview of my services from former clients. Sometimes, former coworkers can be great referral sources, too.

Another favorite referral source is people in adjacent businesses (they're not direct competitors, and referring to you can help round out their offerings). For instance, realtors often refer title companies, mortgage brokers, home inspectors, and a whole host of contractors.

Advertising. You may need to advertise your services to win clients. Whether you advertise through social media or traditional media, ensuring your messages align with your personal brand and speak to the value you provide will be at the top of your list. And just like referrals, testimonials from former clients (and their success stories) can be hugely persuasive messages.

Networking. I almost hesitate to put this on the list… nobody (and do I mean *nobody*) likes to be sold to during networking opportunities. But if you use networking as a relationship-building opportunity that's a precursor to either thought leadership or referrals, it can be <chef's kiss>.

Never try to sell someone you're networking with. Ever. It's about getting to know the other person. And if they're your ideal client, use the networking opportunity to ask them questions that could help build your ideal client avatar (more in Chapter 2). No selling. I mean it.

You're in charge of your own discovery. You've got to let people know. You must tell your ideal clients. And as uncomfortable as this work is, *nobody else can do it for you.*

CONFIDENCE

Ah, yes! The old, "I'll just wait until I'm good and ready," saw. Guess what? The confidence comes *after* you do the thing, not before. It's almost impossible to be confident doing something scary you've never done before. At least it is for non-narcissists.

Preparation and practice are great (and very important), but they don't inherently make you confident. Just ask any performer. It's fundamentally different to do a dress rehearsal than it is to perform in front of a paying audience for the first time. It's an expected part of the process.

Don't think for one minute that you're going to be completely confident going into your first sales or pricing conversation. You won't be. (And that's okay.)

But after you've had some successful conversations like these, you will *become* more confident. And as you gain experience in different selling and pricing situations, you'll learn more, and become even more self-assured.

You've got to do it scared. At least the first time!

When it comes right down to it, people often wait for *themselves*. Waiting to be certain, waiting to become your own advocate, waiting to put yourself out there, or waiting to feel confident and sure about what you're doing.

What I want you to know is that every single one of those hesitations is within your control. Go. Get. After. It.

PRO TIPS

- With much of the work in this book, you may find yourself hesitating or waiting to move forward.
- Don't wait for perfection. It's never going to be perfect; just get it done and get it out there.
- Don't wait for permission. Take charge and set your own agenda. Especially around pricing your services.
- Don't wait for discovery. Your great work needs a voice — advertise and publicize.
- Don't wait for confidence. Do things scared, and your confidence will come.
- Realize that you actually have control over most of the things that make people hesitate. *You* are the person you've been waiting for.

Chapter 21

Managing Your Energy

O kay, when I say "managing your energy," I'm not really talking chakras and woo stuff (although that may be a critical piece of your own preparation).

What I'm talking about is your physical energy and your brain energy. Which are crucial to your success as a service provider, however you think about it.

YOU'RE THE PRODUCT

When you have a service-based consulting or freelance job, you almost always *are* the product, to some extent. That may mean using your creativity, your attention, your skills, your knowledge, or a combination of any or all of them on behalf of your client.

And guess what? All of those activities require a lot of energy. Even when you love what you're doing, and even when you're super-great at it, and even when you've done it a bunch of times before.

It is fundamentally different to sell and price your own products and services than someone else's. And bottom line, it takes more of your energy when you're the product. Don't sell yourself short, money-wise or energy-wise.

YOU'RE SELLING YOUR ENERGY

The reason clients pick service providers isn't only about their qualifications — it has a ton to do with their vibe and how they show up.

Think about a service provider you really like working with, whether it's a stylist, an accountant, a coach, an attorney, a designer, or a consultant. A lot of people have the technical qualifications for the service you're looking at, right? The differentiator is often their energy.

And as a service provider yourself, think about what it's like to be "on" or in a flow state with your client. It's really tough to get into that space without strong physical and mental energy, however that shows up for you.

Your clients want (and need) for you to be energetically present with them. That's what they pay you for. And if you find yourself with so many clients that you're spent and cannot be present, it's probably time to raise your prices so you can afford to work with fewer clients and give them the energy they need.

YOU MUST PRESERVE YOUR ENERGY

Some of the most important work you can do for yourself is to notice what kinds of things you need to do in order to preserve your precious energy so you can use it in service of your clients and your business.

One of the best ways to use your energy most effectively is to be intentional about what you're doing, and when you're doing it. Are you at your best first thing in the morning? Late at night? Somewhere in between? Schedule those tasks that require your freshest brain for when you're most likely to be at your peak.

I have a handful of tasks for my business that require less energy. I earmark those for times when I'm not at my energetic best, but I still want to get things done. A friend calls this "productive procrastination," but I just call it good sense!

It is fundamentally different to sell and price your own products and services than someone else's.

When you've got things to do that will expend a lot of energy (like giving a talk, or facilitating a client session, or whatever you find energy-depleting), be sure to schedule recovery time into your calendar. And don't apologize for needing it.

If you are in creation mode, either because it's the nature of your work or because you're making new products or services on behalf of your business, pay particular attention to your energy. As author Elizabeth Gilbert says, "Creativity is sensitive and needs protection."

It may take some experimentation to find out what works best for you, in terms of energy expenditure, but when you're conscious of how you work and recover best, you'll be not only more efficient, you'll be more effective.

ENERGY DEPLETION AND BURNOUT

One of the most common roadblocks freelancers and consultants face is energy depletion. It may creep up on you, and all of a sudden you find yourself more tired than usual. Or you get interruptions in your sleep patterns. Or you need an extra bit of caffeine to rev yourself up in the morning.

Pay attention to these signs — and do something about them — or you could be headed for burnout.

Make no mistake: burnout isn't just for corporate drones. When you consistently pour out your energy for your clients without taking time off to fill back up, burnout will eventually follow. And it takes way more time to come back from a burnout space than it does from simple depletion.

If you think your clients can't feel your lack of energy, you're wrong. They totally can. And the more depleted you are, the more they can tell. They may not be able to put a finger on what's wrong, but they feel it.

HOW TO RECHARGE YOUR ENERGY

Typical energy-rechargers include time off from work and self-care, but everyone is different. Make yourself a list of what fills your cup. For me, it's a walk in the park (literally!), talking with my kids, taking time with my family, or playing with my dog.

It's especially easy for service providers to be so focused on being available for client work that we don't take time off. Put time off into its proper perspective: it's an important part of recharging your energy so that you can better serve your clients.

And plan well in advance for your time away from the office. Block your calendar, and protect that time from being scheduled over. Take your damned vacations, people!

I would also argue that you can't fully recharge unless you commit to not taking client calls or doing work on behalf of your clients during that time. You can decide for yourself when and if you would take an "emergency" call from a client. If you have your parameters set up front, it'll make those boundaries clear for your clients, and even more importantly, for yourself.

And speaking of boundaries, one of the simplest ways to protect your time is to proactively manage your calendar. I have an online scheduling software for my clients to self-schedule calls with me. I've set things up so clients can't schedule outside of my normal business hours, and I block my Friday afternoons to take care of non-client business.

The default is that clients schedule within those boundaries I've set. Sure, I occasionally work with clients outside of those times, but both the client and I know that it's the exception, not the rule.

PRO TIPS

- Managing your energy is a crucial part of freelance and consulting work; clients want, need, and hire you for your energetic presence.
- Planning your work to match up with your energy patterns will help make you more efficient.
- Your clients can tell when your energy is low, even if they don't know exactly what might be wrong.
- Plan time off and know the best ways to recharge your energy; both are critical to your business.
- Create strong boundaries around your work time, and make it easy for your clients to see and respect them.

Chapter 22
Mindset Q&A

Q: There are tons of experts out there doing what I do, and I'm just now starting my business. Why shouldn't I be pricing my services lower than those other people?

A: When you are just starting out in your specialty area, you may want to price your services on the lower end of the market. If, though, you're new to having your own business, but you're building it on a foundation of working in your specialty for someone else, you may be missing out. Focus on the value you can bring to your clients.

Q: Just the thought of having a conversation with my client about raising my prices makes me sick to my stomach. How can I make things easier on myself?

A: Don't barf! This is a normal and regular part of your business. Make a script with everything you want to say, and practice it — out loud — with a partner. Then, take a few minutes before your pricing conversation to sit quietly and think about how you want to show up, and then go. You've got this!

Q: I'm worried that my client will think I have no business charging as much as I do. How can I get past this?

A: Recognize this is not a client problem; it's a you problem. And remember this isn't personal; it's a business transaction. You don't have to justify your rates — you just have to help your client understand the value of your services.

Q: Won't potential clients get turned off if my website and marketing materials aren't perfect?

A: Perfection is a myth, so no. The type of services you offer will dictate what your website and marketing materials should focus on. If you're a graphic artist, your marketing materials need to reflect your design esthetic.

Management consultants may want to provide articles and resources tied to their subject matter expertise. Dog groomers might focus on before and after photos of their clients.

Regardless of your services, though, everything you do from a website and marketing perspective reflects your own brand, so be sure it all looks professional and has been proofread.

Q: I love my work, but I have so many things going on, I'm really tired when I'm meeting with my clients. What should I do?

A: A couple of things: do a "time audit," and consider raising your prices. With a time audit, you'll look at how you're spending your time every day. How much of it is direct service to your clients? How much is service to your business? How much time is "other"? (You may need to consciously reduce your "other" time.)

If you've got decent time management habits, raising your rates so you can serve fewer clients could be a great answer.

PART 4
PUTTING IT ALL TOGETHER

Now that you have all the elements you need to price your services and set your terms (Toolset, Skillset, and Mindset), let's put everything together and put it into action.

What's in this section…

Chapter 23: Preparing for Client Conversations

Getting ready for your important client conversations including preparing your materials, approach, tools, mind, and exit.

Chapter 24: Expecting the Unexpected

How to handle some of the most common unexpected circumstances including when the engagement runs long, circumstances with you or your client change, or technology changes.

Chapter 25: Just Say No

You're not for everyone. When you should say "no" to working with a client. How to say "no" gracefully.

Chapter 26: When to Revisit Your Pricing

Refreshing your rates regularly, when you create a new service, when you get too busy, and when you encounter a big change.

Chapter 27: Publishing Your Pricing

The pros and cons of publishing your pricing.

Chapter 28: You're Done, Now What?

What you should do when you're done with an important client conversation including tying up loose ends, cutting your losses, learning from your experiences, and celebrating.

Chapter 29: Putting it All Together Q&A

Questions I get about topics in the Putting it All Together section (and how I answer them).

Chapter 23

Preparing for Client Conversations

W hat do you need to have ready before a client conversation about sales, pricing, or terms?

Lots! The great news is that you can — and need to — prepare well ahead of time.

PREPARE YOUR MATERIALS

You've spent a lot of time thinking about your services, how to price them, and what terms you offer. Don't trip at the finish line by not having them at your fingertips!

Before you get on a call or in a meeting with a client, be sure you have your proposal, your package information, your terms, or whatever you might need easily at hand.

In some cases, that will mean printing everything out in hard copy; other situations may work better with just having the documents up on a computer screen.

If you have prepared scripts (which I always think is a great idea), be sure to have them available, too. But know them well enough that you don't read them like some weirdo robot.

And to check yourself, you can always do a quick video recording of yourself on your phone or on Zoom.

PREPARE YOUR APPROACH

To approach your conversations with confidence, I recommend a "sandwich cookie" approach: start and end on a positive note, with the guts of the conversation in the middle.

That middle part can look quite different in a pricing conversation than in a sale to an individual, but expressing delight at the beginning and ending the conversation on an up note are both crucial. Don't skip them!

1. **Express delight.** Make sure your client knows that you're thrilled to be talking with them about the opportunity to help them with your services. Whether you're consulting or freelancing, this step is important. No matter what type of conversation you have, starting on a positive note sets the stage well.

2. **The middle.** This piece will be different for each type of conversation you might have. Here are a few samples:

    - *Sale to individual.* Ask them what made them get on a call with you (you're listening for the problem they're trying to solve). Ask what the solution would mean to them (ties into their values). Only then will you start telling them about your services and how you can help them. And don't start serving them before you've closed the sale and received your up-front payment. (Coaches: that means *no coaching* on the sales call!)

    - *Sale to corporate client.* I'm thinking of this one as the discussion you have with your potential client to discuss your prepared freelance or consulting proposal with them. You'll go over your proposal, step by step. Listen closely; you may get feedback that will warrant some changes to your agreements.

- *Price increase.* Talk with the client about what the price increase will be, when it will happen, and any early sign-up enticements you're offering.

- *Negotiating terms.* Let your client know what your terms are, ask for clarification on their requests (this is not the time to get defensive), and propose solutions. If you need time to review the client's proposed terms with your attorney, ask for it, and set a time to follow up.

3. **End on an up note.** Finishing with a positive statement and sentiment is always a good practice. Express confidence that you'll be able to come to terms you both agree on, or let them know you're sure they'll make the right decision for them, or tell them how much you value their business. Aim for calm, self-assured, and optimistic. Steer away from desperate, grabby, or begging language — it won't help you or your client.

Once you map out how you'd like the conversation to go, create scripts (more in Chapter 16), and practice them. Out loud. A lot.

PREPARE YOUR TOOLS

By tools, I mean your phone, your computer, and stuff you need so you can take notes.

If you'll be on a phone call, be sure your battery is charged, your phone notifications are off, and you're in a place where you get great reception. If you'll be on a videoconference, shut down all of the windows and applications you're not using, make sure you have strong internet service, and turn off all of the annoying notification dings from email, your calendar, and your phone. If you're talking with a client in person, again, turn off notifications on your phone.

I always recommend that you have a glass of water with you, and paper and pen or pencil to take notes (and give yourself a couple of pens, just in case one runs out — it happens). And don't forget the materials you've prepped (see above).

And if things don't go the way you expect (The power goes off! Your internet stops working!), be flexible and have a sense of humor. Remember, every interaction with your client is an opportunity to show them how great it would be to work with you.

PREPARE YOUR MIND

One of the very best things you can do to prepare for client conversations is to get your brain in order. And by that, I mean meditate.

Some folks don't think meditation and business go together. I do! While I consider myself to be pragmatic and business-focused, I am a huge fan of using meditation to prepare for challenging conversations, especially sales and pricing ones. These types of discussions are some of the toughest ones we have in business.

If you already have a meditation practice, use that to prepare. If you don't, or just can't stomach the idea of meditation, just sit quietly for a bit, and think about as little as possible. You can employ box breathing (inhale to a count of four, hold your breath for a count of four, exhale for a count of four, hold your breath for a count of four) to slow things down for yourself, too.

Once you've taken a few minutes to settle your mind, take another couple to focus on how you want to show up. You'll enter your conversation calmer and more relaxed.

My clients tell me that even a five-minute session of meditation or quiet reflection helps them focus and be present for important conversations like these.

PREPARE YOUR EXIT: GOOD OR BAD

Be prepared for the next step, regardless of the outcome of the conversation.

The good. What will you do when the client says "yes"? Believe it or not, this is a step that many service providers miss preparing for, and there's a wild scramble every time. You absolutely must be prepared for how to end the conversation and be certain about what comes next.

It could be a "Congratulations!" note to your client detailing their package. It could be sending your client an agreement to e-sign, and then an invoice afterwards. If your clients will be self-scheduling, make sure to send a link. Make a system for yourself with a checklist of things to do (and in what order) plus templates for your communications.

You might also want to share something with your client that reinforces their decision to work with you. One of my favorite ways to share with my clients is to offer blog posts or articles I've written that relate to the topic we'll be working on together.

If things don't go the way you expect, be flexible and have a sense of humor.

Just don't start working before you receive your up-front payment (more in Chapter 13).

The bad. Not every sales, renewal, pricing, or terms conversation will go the way you hope. Sometimes, your services are not going to be a match with what the client is looking for. And every once in a blue moon, you might run into a client you just know you don't want to work with.

One thing that will likely make you less nervous about running into a situation like this is to plan for what you'll say and do.

How will you approach it? Do you want to down-sell in this case? Or refer? Or thank them for their time and send them on their way? Make yourself a script and practice it. You'll be much more likely to have a graceful exit when you know exactly how you will approach the situation.

Even something as simple as, "I appreciate the opportunity to work with you on the proposal. Now that I've learned more about the project, it's clear to me the project will take more time than I can commit in the next month <or whatever it is that makes it not a good fit>, so I'll need to bow out" can be helpful.

Of course, the title of the movie is "The Good, The Bad, and the Ugly," but I'm skipping the ugly part. Because you've done such a great job of preparing yourself, and you're not taking it personally, the likelihood of an ugly outcome is pretty darned remote!

PRO TIPS

- Bring all of your materials and scripts together before your conversation so all your critical information is within easy reach.
- Know exactly how you want the conversation to unfold, and begin and end your discussion on a positive note.
- Take your time to make sure your computer, phone, internet, and any other tools you need to have a great conversation are ready to go.
- Before you jump on a call (or meet) with a client, take a few minutes and meditate or sit quietly. When you're done, think about how you want to show up so you're focused and intentional.
- If your conversation doesn't go the way you hoped, be prepared for how to bow out gracefully. It can have a bigger impact on your brand than you may think.

Chapter 24

Expecting the Unexpected

Sometimes, things don't go according to plan. But that doesn't mean you can't prepare in advance. The more you've considered the most common ways things can go sideways, the more likely you can be nimble when they happen.

THE ENGAGEMENT RUNS LONG

This is one of the most common things to have happen when you're a consultant or freelancer. So plan for it.

One of the best things you can do is to make sure any additional deliverables or expansion in scope are comprehended in your agreements. Have a clear and frank conversation with your client at the first sign the engagement might go beyond what you first expected.

How do they want to approach things? Are they ready for you to put an addendum together? What should it include? What if they need to halt at the end of the original time period due to budget reasons? How could you wind things down then?

It can be challenging to predict what your client might do in this situation, so have at least a couple of alternatives in your back pocket before speaking with your client.

CIRCUMSTANCES WITH YOUR CLIENT CHANGE

Sometimes, your client's circumstances will change. They may have something urgent that comes up and pushes timelines back. Or they might have a shift in their financial situation. Or a key contact at the company changes. Or they may even ghost you.

It's important to consider what the types of changes of circumstance are most likely for your clients — you may need to add items into your agreements, just in case.

For instance, if your client needs to push out your timeline and deliverables, how far could they do that without having a material impact on your business? Would you want to have some sort of clause in your agreements that requires a renegotiation after a set period of time?

However your circumstances impact your clients, the one thing you can do is focus on the best way to serve your clients through them.

If your key contact changes, what needs to happen to get them up to speed? If you would need to provide additional services in order for the client to move forward with the engagement, work with the client to define them (and put an addendum with additional pricing together).

It's unlikely that a client will simply stop communicating with you, but it can occasionally happen. And sometimes, it's for the same types of reasons in the "Your Circumstances Change" section below.

But if a client isn't providing the timely feedback you need to complete your deliverables, it can be a challenge. Communicate directly and firmly with your client, letting them know that you won't be able to complete the work you agreed on without their input and/or approval. You may also want to consider including wording in your agreements about this, too.

And if a client becomes unable to pay, will it be appropriate to stop providing services and allow your client to simply not pay anything additional? How might your policy change if the client had already received their services and then couldn't pay? You can talk with your attorney and your accountant (more in Chapter 8) for tips on how you could handle these situations if they came up.

YOUR CIRCUMSTANCES CHANGE

What if things with you change? Depending on the type of work you do and where you are in your career, you may experience changes that can impact your clients.

(And just in case you think these kinds of things never happen, I've brought my own clients and business through all the cases below except for change of control.)

Illness or injury. You or a family member may have a short-term illness, a sudden injury, or a debilitating illness or injury that prevents you from working altogether. You may need to re-negotiate deadlines or meetings, or exit completely from your engagement, depending on your situation.

Whatever the case, do your best to clearly communicate with your client, and have a crisis management plan in case you're not able to communicate directly with your clients yourself.

Moving. A physical move of your business may or may not impact your clients. When I moved my consulting practice from California to Texas (pre-Oregon), I fully expected to lose most of my California clients, since I wouldn't be able to meet on site easily. To my surprise (and delight), my clients kept me on, because our long-term working relationships made it easy for us to work together remotely.

If you're not able to serve your existing clients well from your new location, work to help them find new solutions. And if you can continue to work with your clients from another location, be sure to thank them for their continued business.

Closing business. You may decide to stop offering certain services, retire, or gain employment elsewhere, and close your business (or at least part of it). In these cases, it's important to end your relationship with your clients well.

Are there others you can refer your clients to? Do you have files that would benefit the client after your engagement ends? Remember your legacy, and do your best to create good closure with your client.

Change of control. If you sell your business or go into partnership with someone else, chances are good that part of what you're selling is your book of business. If you stay with the business, it's likely that your client won't see much of a difference.

If you exit the business, though, make sure you're offering your client a warm handoff to whoever will be taking over their account. It's one of the best things you can do to ensure your client continues to receive good service.

However your circumstances impact your clients, the one thing you can do is focus on the best way to serve your clients through them. Careful planning and advance notice — to the extent you are able — will give your clients the best experience possible.

TECHNOLOGY CHANGES

With technology changes, I'm primarily referring to your technology, like a training platform, website/URL, scheduling software, billing processes, and the like.

The great thing about technology changes is that you can minimize their impact on your clients with careful and abundant communication. They will need to know what is changing and when, how the change impacts them, and what actions they need to take.

The more complex the changes, the more likely you will need help from a communications expert. Don't hesitate to hire someone to help you make a user guide or to write a clear memo to your clients explaining the exact steps they will need to take.

PRO TIPS

- Sometimes, circumstances change that can impact the way you serve your clients. Think about how you might handle things in advance to serve your clients well.

- Engagements sometimes run long. The key to managing the extended timeline is clear communication, both up front in your agreement, and once you realize that the engagement may go longer than expected.

- Your client may have situations come up that change the nature of your work together. If their circumstances create additional work for you, be sure to recognize — and charge — for it.

- Your circumstances may change and impact how you deliver services to your clients. Plan in advance how you might handle these changes and focus on your client's experience.

- Communicate well and often if you have changes in technology that impact your clients.

Chapter 25

Just Say No

You and your services are not for everyone. So don't feel bad if a client isn't a fit for you, whatever the reason might be. They may not select you, or you may decide to say no to them.

YOU ARE NOT FOR EVERYONE (AND THAT'S PERFECT)

If you've done the work you need to in establishing your value and niche (more in Chapter 2), it will be clear to you that your services aren't for everyone. *Nor should they be.* So be very sure you're not trying to appeal to people or organizations that aren't aligned with your ideal client profile.

It's easy to fall into a "likability trap," where you want everyone to like you and want your services. One of the most important things you can do is to not be generically likable.

That's not to say you shouldn't be pleasant, but don't try to win over people you don't actually want to sell to. It will water down the messages that your ideal client really wants to hear.

For example, if you're a stylist who specializes in neon hair color, you're selling to clients who dig neon hair color. Not to people who would never contemplate pink or green hair. You probably don't want to spend a lot of energy and waste your time trying to convince "never-neons" that they should try the brights, either. It's okay to let them go. Be all the way out there — sing the song of neon — so your people can find you.

If you moderate your messages in order to market your services more generically, you may very well miss the boat with clients who actually want and need your uniqueness.

WHEN YOU SHOULD SAY "NO"

It can feel counterintuitive when you've been working hard to establish your business, but there are times when you absolutely should not work with a client.

If the client won't accept your terms. Some clients don't want to pay the prices you've established. That's okay. I had a guy who told me that my prices were ten times what he thought I should charge (and he thought I should charge that lower amount and take him on as a client). That was a hard pass (and even harder eye-roll) for me.

Sometimes, you'll run across a potential client who wants to rework agreements to the point that they're not acceptable to you. You might find that they want your time exclusively dedicated to them (but you don't), they aren't in a position to accept your pricing, they want the intellectual property rights (and you want to keep them), or a host of other things.

When a client is unable or refuses to meet your terms, it's not a failure on your part — or theirs. It's a misalignment. When a business transaction is not a match, that's *business*. It is not personal. It's okay. And frankly it's *way* better to find out before you start an engagement with them than after.

Some clients have an outsized reaction to certain terms and conditions in your agreements. Say "no" to those, too.

When I hear clients having a big reaction to something like a cancellation policy or payment terms, I'm always a bit wary.

My experience is that clients sometimes react in places where they've had (or created) issues with other vendors before, so it makes sense to pay close attention.

Your services aren't for everyone. *Nor should they be.*

If the service isn't in your wheelhouse. It's so easy to say "yes" when a client asks if you can do something that's not on your services list (You love working with them! It's more money!). But it's important to be able to say "no" at the right times, too.

When you want to be known as an expert in one area, accepting engagements outside that area can dilute your impact in your chosen field. If you want to be known as a generalist, that's not necessarily bad.

But it can be if you want to specialize. And if the request is outside of your core area of expertise, you might not be able to deliver at the same level of quality to your client as you can with your specialty, which could impact your reputation.

Being scattershot with your services can impact your energy, too. It can be challenging to shift from one area to the next, especially as you're establishing your business. Remember, just like you're not for every client, you're also not for every service.

If the client doesn't treat you well. Some clients are jerks. Some without meaning to be; some who actually do (or simply don't care if they are). Just say "no" to these folks.

Whether the client is slow to pay (or won't pay at all), they're not willing to do the work they need to in order to get the results they want, or they're outright rude, you don't have to tolerate their bad behavior.

If they're already your client, address any issues you have with them head on (Chapter 7 has more on this), but think twice about extending their contracts or working with them again.

If you get to a point where things are so massively uncomfortable you want to break your agreement with your client, talk with your attorney first to better understand your rights and obligations under the terms of your existing agreement.

If you're so close that you can't remain objective. There's a reason doctors aren't allowed to treat family members. And the same might hold true for you, too, especially if you're in an advisory field. Objectivity — on both sides — is an essential component of many services.

It can be tempting to provide services to close friends and family, but think about what might happen if they didn't get the results they wanted from your time together. Could your relationship stand that strain? If not (or even if you're not sure), consider referring them to someone else.

If you just don't feel right about it. Eventually, you'll run into a potential client your gut tells you not to work with. Listen to your gut.

In my salary negotiation practice, some potential clients think they should be able to negotiate my rates, and want to treat it like a game. I don't. Some think my rates are too high and want to berate me into lowering them. I won't. (That's not to say I don't offer special pricing for specific types of engagements; see Chapter 12.)

Pay close attention to signs like these that the potential client is not respecting you and/or your practice: there can be big (and unpleasant) knock-on consequences.

This lack of respect can translate into a number of bad client behaviors, like being late or unprepared, cancelling meetings, slow/no pay, trying to renegotiate terms mid-engagement, or a host of special requests that can cost you time and/or money.

In a worst-case scenario, a client like this might even try underhanded manipulation (like the threat of poor reviews or negative social media comments) to get you to cave to their demands. While I've been fortunate to never experience this sort of thing personally, I know others who have, and it's every bit as unpleasant as it sounds.

Bottom line: when a potential client shows their bad behavior even before you get to the agreement stage, don't let them graduate into full-fledged, pain-in-the-butt clients. Take Maya Angelou's advice: "When people show you who they are, believe them the first time."

SAYING "NO" GRACEFULLY

It's always a great idea to help people find solutions to their problems, even when you're not it. Like the Santa in "Miracle on 34th Street" who sent shoppers to a competitor when the store he worked in was out of stock, you'll get a reputation as a trusted source.

A prospect who doesn't convert into a client today might refer someone else to you, or they might be in a position to become a client down the road. There are great tips on down-selling and referring in Chapter 14.

You will, at some point, have to say "no" to a client. You owe it to yourself to outline what kinds of common situations or conditions will trigger the just-say-no response — and what exactly you'll do about it — before they happen.

PRO TIPS

- You (and your services) aren't for everybody. Don't try to be.
- If you try to appeal to everyone, you may be turning off people who *are* in your niche. Talk directly to your ideal clients, and don't worry about everyone else.
- There are times you shouldn't work with a client. If they can't meet your terms, don't treat you well, you can't be objective with them, or if things don't feel right, just say "no."
- It's important to treat folks you won't be working with well, too. They could wind up becoming clients or referring business to you.
- Know what you'll say "no" to (and what you'll do about it) before it happens.

Chapter 26

When to Revisit Your Pricing

It can feel overwhelming to think about revisiting your rates when you've just reworked your pricing. Plan how you want to approach pricing changes for your business so the decision isn't hanging over your head all the time.

REGULAR RATE REFRESHES

As a part of your strategic planning for your business, you need to review your pricing to make sure it still makes sense, and make any adjustments you'd like to.

When you're just starting out, you may need to adjust things multiple times over the first year, but after that, a semi-annual or annual refresh may work well for you.

Some service providers even like to make changes more frequently than that, but I'd personally find that a bit exhausting, since I have a large suite of services.

WHEN YOU CREATE A NEW SERVICE

Of course, any time you create a new service offering, you'll need to figure out how much to charge. When your new service goes with other packages or services you offer, you also need to think about how everything hangs together. If anything needs adjusting, you can make all the changes at once.

If you're consulting or selling services to businesses, you might find that a new proposal method or terms or add-on services works great. You could decide to switch things up for future clients and/or renewals, which might shift your pricing.

WHEN YOU GET TOO BUSY

Oh, sure! You're already too busy, and now is the time to raise your rates?

Absolutely!

But won't some existing clients leave? Yes, they will. And that can be a good thing.

Plan how you want to approach pricing changes for your business so the decision isn't hanging over your head all the time.

Sometimes, clients keep you stuck in the status quo, especially around pricing. It's not like people run around and beg to pay more for something.

But as your practice evolves, the value you can bring to your clients often does, too. If your current clients are not in a place to realize that elevated value, they may not want to pay for it, either. And that is absolutely okay. Remember, your services are not for everyone.

Knowing your services are in high demand can give you the confidence you need to bring your pricing up. In these cases, it can actually benefit you (and your other clients) to have some clients leave your practice and open up time on your overstuffed calendar.

What would that additional time do for you? For your business? For your clients?

It could be really awesome, right?

WHEN SOMETHING BIG CHANGES

If something big happens with your business, it makes sense to think about how your pricing could and should change. Whether it's taking on a partner, changing suppliers, or a major competitor dropping out of the marketplace, you may find ways your pricing needs to shift at the same time.

PRO TIPS

- Set a schedule of regular pricing refreshes when you do your strategic planning.
- When you create and price a new service, see how the new service coordinates with your existing services and pricing, and make any needed adjustments.
- If you're busier than you would like to be in your business, consider raising your rates. Losing clients is part of that bargain, and it can serve your business well.
- Big changes in your business should come with consideration of how your pricing needs to change, too.

Chapter 27

Publishing Your Pricing

P eople ask me all the time whether or not they should publish the prices for their services. My answer? It depends.

HOW PUBLISHING YOUR PRICING CAN *HURT* YOU

Screening good clients out. When you publish your pricing on your website, you may inadvertently screen out folks who could be great clients. These potential customers might think, "yikes, I can't afford it," or "gee, it doesn't seem worth it," and exit the sales process before you even get to talk with them.

It can be challenging to communicate value to potential clients through a website (although there are some who do a great job in this space).

Making extra work. When you haven't quite settled on your pricing, it can be a bit of a pain to revise your website and other pieces of collateral every time you decide to tweak things.

If you're not quite sure what pricing you'll settle on, or if you are in the middle of changing your prices, you may want to hold off on publishing them until you land the final numbers.

HOW PUBLISHING YOUR PRICING CAN *HELP* YOU

Market positioning. If it's the norm for people who do what you do to publish their pricing, you may want to, too. When it's easy to compare service pricing, it's important to share your value proposition (more in Chapter 2) at the same time so potential clients can see how you position yourself in the market.

Qualification. I now publish my pricing for my salary negotiation coaching on my website, although I didn't always. It was only after having several "get acquainted calls" in a row where potential clients balked at my pricing that I changed my tune.

The service I offer is unique enough that potential clients don't really have a good frame of reference as to what it should cost. I feel like I'm doing them a service to make those prices publicly available so they can think it over a bit before talking with me.

Should you publish your prices? It depends.

Frankly, I don't want to waste my time or that of a potential client if they already have an idea in their head about what's an appropriate amount to pay, and my fees are above that. I do offer some success stories right above the pricing table on my website, so that helps people understand the value of the service I offer, too.

These days, virtually every potential client I talk with has seen my pricing table before we get on a call. For me, it's made things easier, but it may not be the same for everyone.

Bottom line, you will need to make a decision on whether or not to publish your pricing. If you just can't figure it out, though, I'd recommend holding off on publishing if you are just starting out. You may find it helpful to be super-clear about your value before taking that leap.

PRO TIPS

- Some people publish their prices; others don't. You'll have to decide for yourself which practice serves you and your business best.
- Keeping your prices unpublished can help you if you need a personal touch to help people understand the value you bring to your clients, or if you're still refining how to price your services.
- Publishing your prices can help clarify your position in the market, and it can also help you make sure that potential clients who do meet with you are more likely to be okay with your prices.

Chapter 28

You're Done, Now What?

Whew. That's a lot to think about!

You've figured out your value, set your prices, figured out your terms, decided what to say, managed your energy, had challenging conversations with your clients, and so much more.

So, what happens next?

TIE UP LOOSE ENDS

After any major conversation with a client about sales, pricing, or terms, it's normal to be tired. Exhausted, even. But don't let the follow up to the conversation slide.

Have you created new terms that need to be modified in the agreement? Make the changes, and get that new version out, pronto.

Changed your pricing? Put the details in writing, and send an email to your client, documenting your conversation.

Closed a sale? Send your invoice for your up-front payment. I also recommend sending your client something that cements your new relationship, like an article reprint, a book, an assessment, or anything that taps into the excitement of your engagement (and it's okay to wait to send anything that costs you money until their first payment arrives).

CUT YOUR LOSSES...GRACEFULLY

If you need to bow out (more in Chapter 25), or if you don't win the sale, be gracious about it. Even when you're not moving forward with the engagement, you are still creating a brand experience with the person you're interacting with. And it might lead to business down the line. You never know.

Stay classy, everybody!

> Celebrating — in a way that's meaningful to you — plays an important role in ensuring your future successes.

LEARN FROM YOUR EXPERIENCES

Experience is a powerful teacher. (So powerful that I was moved to write a book to spare you from as many of the mistakes I've made as possible and to help you benefit from learning things that worked well for me.)

Keep track of your challenges and your opportunities. What happened that you want to repeat over and over? What will you never, ever do again?

A great practice to adopt is sitting down after every conversation you have with a client about sales, pricing, or terms, and think about what you're learning about your services, your clients, and yourself. Write it all down, and put it where you can find it again. Refer to this treasure trove of information early and often, and incorporate what you've learned into your next client conversation or service design.

CELEBRATE YOUR SUCCESSES

Celebrating — in a way that's meaningful to you — plays an important role in ensuring your future successes. When you celebrate, it's fun, sure, but you're also training your brain to reinforce those neural pathways so you can do that awesome thing again (and maybe even more easily next time).

Don't skip over it because you're too busy or you weren't perfect or for some other lame reason. Give your soul the happy reinforcement it craves.

It's science-y to celebrate!

PRO TIPS

- As soon you're done with any big client "thing," follow up on any paperwork and client care that's needed.
- If things don't work out with a client, your gracious exit from the process can reinforce your great reputation.
- The time you take reflecting on your experiences — both good and bad — can pay off big time with your future client interactions.
- Celebration is not just fun, it's necessary.

Chapter 29
Putting it All Together Q&A

Q: Why can't I combine a proposal and a retainer into a single service for my client?
A: You totally can. As long as it's not confusing to your client and you can keep track of everything from an administrative perspective, it can be helpful to get creative when you're helping your client solve problems.

Q: It takes a ton of time to prepare a proposal and a consulting agreement. Can I charge the client for that?
A: Sort of. Be sure to comprehend that time in the final costs. You could also consider making the assessment and planning work into a project phase of its own and charging for that. Also, be sure you're giving a sketch, not a portrait.

Q: What should I do when I lose a client because I've raised my prices?
A: Treat it as a healthy part of your business growth. Because it is. Some clients will stick with you through price increases, and some won't.

Q: I've been working with a potential corporate client for a month now, trying to get them to accept my consulting proposal. How can I move them along?
A: It can be frustrating when a client takes forever to make a decision on a proposal! Your ability to move them along in the process may be limited by things that are going on inside the organization, which are beyond your control. That said, you can ask them to make a choice between

moving forward with the proposal now or tabling it for a couple of weeks (or months). That may help them move into decision mode.

Q: My partner just got a job in another city, and we've decided to move. How do I tell my clients?

A: Just as soon as you have a plan on how you'll handle your business with the move (refer to other providers, shift to remote service, etc.), let your clients know what's happening. It may be no big deal to them, or it could have a huge impact. Give your clients as much notice as you can, and work hard to make the transition as easy as possible for them.

Q: My client said something wildly inappropriate (and sexual harassment-y) in our meeting to review my proposal. What am I supposed to do now?

A: Strongly reconsider working with the client. This would be a hard "no" for me. And in the proposal stage, it's usually pretty easy to graciously bow out of the process.

Q: I'm not currently publishing my prices on my website, but I keep getting people who are interested in my services who totally freak out over my prices. Should I reconsider?

A: Probably. It doesn't make sense to waste your time or that of potential clients if they think your services should cost far less than they do. It's great to be able to screen those folks out before they talk with you. But you'll probably also want to add in testimonials or case studies that help potential clients understand the value of your services at the same time.

Q: I keep creating proposals, and the clients seem really excited, but then they ghost me. What's wrong?
A: This can be really scary! But look at it as an opportunity to learn more about your business and your proposal process. Remember, this is not personal!

First, are the clients you're meeting with your ideal clients? If they're not, that's actually good news — they're self-selecting out of the process. You'll want to revisit what happens with clients before they get to the proposal stage to figure out how to weed them out earlier in the process.

On the other hand, if the clients you're creating proposals for *are* your ideal clients, take a look at the proposal process itself. How well do you understand the issue your client is trying to solve? How are you articulating your solutions? What's happening in the meetings? What kind of follow-up are you doing? Get curious about everything, and enlist a friend or a coach to help you break things down and see what needs to be changed up.

PART 5

Other Awesome Stuff

Resource Reference Guide

Some of my favorite resources, including books, podcasts, articles, software, and other cool stuff.

Conclusion

Acknowledgements

Index

About the Author

Resource Reference Guide

There are zillions of books, videos, podcasts, articles, blogs, and other content about topics adjacent to the ones we've covered here, but I'd like to recommend a handful of resources here that I particularly like.

BOOKS & ARTICLES

Daring Greatly, by Brené Brown. Creating, running, and growing a service business takes a lot of courage. There's nobody like Brené to help you get your head on straight in this space.

Building a StoryBrand, by Donald Miller. I just love this book! It's super-digestible and has tons of great actionable advice about marketing and positioning. If you want to know more about focusing on your client, read this book.

Catapulting Commissions, by Anthony Garcia. This super-easy read about achieving (and exceeding!) your sales goals is a gold mine of sales mindset tips. I especially love its focus on managing your expectations and energy.

How Customers Think: Essential Insights into the Mind of the Market, by Gerald Zaltman. Interesting, if slightly nerdy, take on how consumers make decisions.

When, by Daniel Pink. There are lots of fascinating findings about time in this book. Much of my advice on starting and ending conversations was influenced by his research on beginnings and endings.

Crucial Conversations, by Patterson, Grenny, McMillan, and Switzler. Great advice about having high-stakes discussions.

PODCASTS & VIDEOS

Become a Thought Leader with Kasey Jones. This YouTube channel features authentic branding guru (and my friend) Kasey Jones. Amazingly helpful, fun, and irreverant content on marketing, mindset, and entrepreneurship.

I especially love her content on podcasting and her book reviews. So good!

ETL (Entrepreneurial Thought Leaders). Part of Stanford's Speaker Series, this wide-ranging podcast covers topics from inclusivity to sustainability to ethics and more.

OTHER RESOURCES

The Kolbe A Index. The Kolbe A Index (it's available at Kolbe.com and at this writing costs $55) looks at your "conative" process, which helps you understand how you approach problem-solving (as opposed to cognitive, which deals with thinking, and affective, which relates to feeling). I love it so much I got certified in it!

Why is this so important? It's an energy thing. Knowing your problem-solving strengths can help you focus your time and energy so you can be more productive. It can also help you understand what sorts of tasks and activities require more of your energy than others.

Small Business Administration. Your US tax dollars fund this government agency — use it! The SBA (sba.gov) has a zillion free resources on setting up your business, marketing, how to become a federal contractor, and more.

Conclusion

This is the end…but it's only the beginning.

I hope you found this book to be of help to you and your business. Even more, I hope you will continue to weave deliberate choices around pricing and policies into the fiber of your business for years to come.

I'm excited for you.

Seeing the difference this work makes for my clients and their businesses gets me pretty excited. In fact, it's the main reason I decided to write this book — to sprinkle that awesomeness far and wide in my quest to empower as many business owners as I can.

I truly believe that the more deliberate decisions you make in your business, the more confident you'll become, and the more fulfilled you'll become with your work. That's been true for me, and it's a game-changer.

I'm confident in you.

I know you can do this. It's hard, but it's worth it. And by taking the time to read and understand everything we've talked about in this book, you're showing a level of commitment to your business — and to yourself.

You've. Got. This.

Thank you so much.

This book has been a labor of love for me, and I'm grateful you've invested your time in reading it!

If you find typos, I'd appreciate it if you'd let me know. As much as my editor and I have worked to correct them, I'm sure there are some. (And in case you're hesitating because you don't want to be the first to give feedback, let me assure you, you won't be.)

Keep in touch!

I absolutely love hearing success stories from my readers! If you've found any of the tips and techniques from *Name Your Price* to be helpful, please drop me a line at info@ katedixon.org.

Did you enjoy the book? If so, I'd be grateful if you left a review on the website of the store you purchased the book from — reviews are vitally important to help readers find and enjoy new books.

For more information about me, to subscribe to my monthly newsletter, or to read more, please visit:

www.katedixon.org/NameYourPriceBook.

Acknowledgements

The journey to create this book has only been possible with the support, guidance, and cheerleading from a whole host of wonderful people.

My colleagues. The extremely fabulous Robyn Bolton and delightful Rashmi Dixit offered heart-centered and candid counsel, and they helped me crystalize thoughts and ideas included in the book.

My reader friends. Huge thanks to my editor, Emily Fuggetta, along with my trusted pals who read and gave feedback on early versions of the book. Gina Riley, Kasey Jones, Monique Montanino, Debi Muchow, Lisa Hunefeld, Nancy Turner, Monefa Anderson, Angelika Olson, Carrie Tannenbaum, Lori Emerick, Sue Parham, and Tammi Wheeler, you're fantastic!

My writer friends. Jess, Jeff, Stephanie, Jenn, Trish, and Hildred, I'm so grateful for your guidance and encouragement.

My family. My parents, Betsy and Will, and my siblings, Jim, Kelly, and Charles have enthusiastically supported me in all sorts of ventures over the years (and Mom's the best proofreader of all time!). My nieces Sophia, Marie, and Katy, and my nephew Riley are each delightful and inspire me daily.

My little dog, Jeffrey, sat unflaggingly beside me (bored, I'm sure) as I wrote.

My amazing kids, Liz and Jay, have been wildly encouraging (and I'm so proud of you both!). My husband, Steve, has quietly supported my writing habit by doing way more than his fair share of the work around the house. (I really did notice!)

Index

About the Author

Kate Dixon, author of ***Name Your Price:*** *Set Your Terms, Raise Your Rates, and Charge What You're Worth as a Consultant, Coach, or Freelancer*, and ***Pay Up!*** *Unlocking Insider Secrets of Salary Negotiation*, is Principal and Founder of **Dixon Consulting**, a leadership development and total rewards consultancy that specializes in salary negotiation and pricing coaching, compensation solutions, as well as workshops and teambuilding for organizations of all sizes, from startups to Fortune 100 companies.

Kate's passion is helping diverse leaders around the world accelerate their results to become more successful and more fulfilled.

Kate has spent the past 25 years working for and consulting with leaders in for-profit companies including Nike, Intel, American Express, Mercari, and Kaiser Permanente, as well as non-profits like The Learning Policy Institute, One Community Health, DePaul Industries, Period, and Northwest Housing Alternatives. She's founded three successful businesses, two of which have been consulting and coaching practices.

She's a professional certified coach, and has been certified in compensation for over 25 years.

Her latest venture, **RaKa Rising**, is a consulting partnership with Rashmi Dixit offering anti-oppressive human resources program design, coaching, and consulting; for more information, please visit **rakarising.com**.

A proud mom of two delightful kids (Liz and Jay), Kate was born in Brooklyn, New York, and has lived all over the United States. She received both her undergraduate and master's degrees from Purdue University, and lives in Portland, Oregon with her husband Steve and their little dog, Jeffrey.

Kate provides advice about pricing, compensation, and leadership to subscribers at **katedixon.org**.

Made in the USA
Monee, IL
17 November 2022

17963411R00136